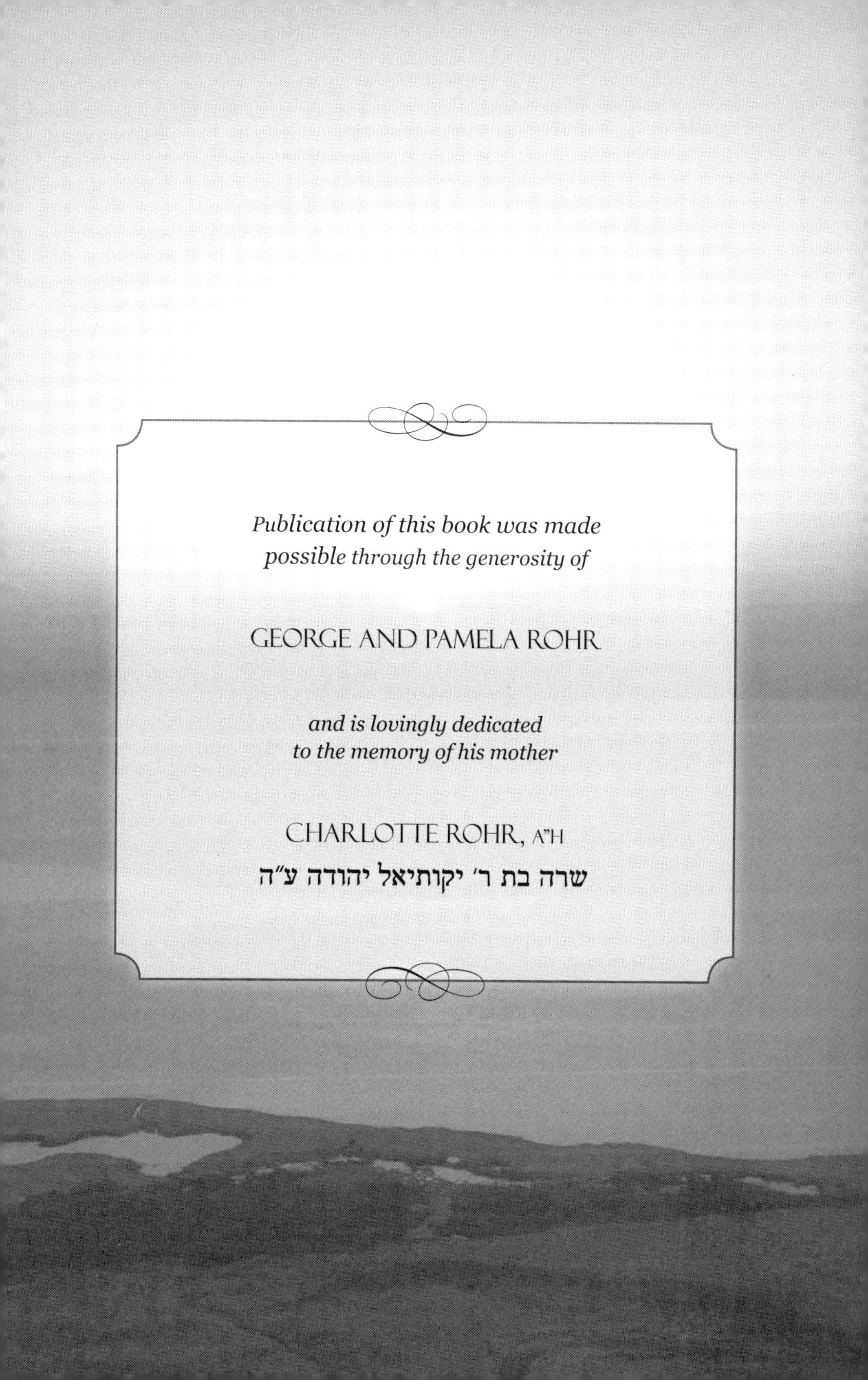

Publication of this book was made possible through the generosity of

GEORGE AND PAMELA ROHR

and is lovingly dedicated to the memory of his mother

CHARLOTTE ROHR, A"H

שרה בת ר׳ יקותיאל יהודה ע״ה

BEYOND SURVIVAL

As a teacher, Shimon Apisdorf contributes a great deal to our synagogue and community. As an author, he inspires Jews around the world. I enjoyed reviewing the manuscript for Beyond Survival *and am sure that Jews of all backgrounds will find it to be a wonderful resource for years to come.*

—Rabbi Menachem Goldberger, Baltimore

In prayer, we use our hearts and souls to climb ever closer to the summit of connection to our Creator. Regardless of how long you have been climbing, Beyond Survival *will serve as an invaluable tool as you strive to discover the riches hidden within the Rosh Hashanah prayers.*

—Rabbi Michel Twerski, Milwaukee

K'hal PUBLISHING

leviathan press
wisdom for the mind, inspiration for the soul™

AFIKIM FOUNDATION

First Edition / First Impression: August 2008

Published by **K'hal Publishing** & **Leviathan Press**
In conjunction with **The Afikim Foundation**
111 John Street, Suite 1720
New York, NY 10038
212-791-7450
www.afikimfoundation.org

Layout & Design	Block Design/blockdesign@gmail.com
Cover Illustration	Joseph Salina, Toronto
Photography	Yuval Nadel, Israel

Distributed by MESORAH PUBLICATIONS, LTD.,
4401 Second Avenue, Brooklyn, NY, 11232 / www.artscroll.com

Distributed in Israel by SIFRIATI/A. GITLER, 6 Hayarkon Street / Bnei Brak 51127

Distributed in Europe by LEHMANNS, Unit E, Viking Business Park,
Rolling Mill Road / Jarrow, Tyne and Wear, NE32 3DP/ England

Distributed in Australia and New Zealand by GOLDS WORLD OF JUDAICA,
3-13 William Street / Balaclava, Melbourne 3183 / Victoria Australia

Distributed in South Africa by KOLLEL BOOKSHOP,
Ivy Common / 105 William Road / Norwood 2192, Johannesburg, South Africa

ISBN: 978-1-60204-012-0 Hardcover
978-1-60204-013-7 Paperback

Printed in the United States of America.

✦ Other books by Shimon Apisdorf

Rosh Hashanah Yom Kippur Survival Kit
The Survival Kit Family Haggadah
Chanukah: Eight Nights of Light, Eight Gifts For the Soul
The One Hour Purim Primer
Kosher For the Clueless But Curious
The Death of Cupid
Judaism In A Nutshell: God
Judaism In A Nutshell: Israel
Judaism In A Nutshell: Holidays
Judaism In A Nutshell: Passover

An insightful guide to experiencing the beautifully deep potential of marriage.

—John Gray, author,
Men Are From Mars, Women Are From Venus

The Rosh Hashanah Yom Kippur Survival Kit will open up the gates of prayer for a new generation.

—Rabbi Dr. Jonathan Sacks, Chief Rabbi of England

Shimon Apisdorf explains in 30 to 60 second sound bites the role Israel has played in the hearts and history of the Jewish people. Will help many understand how Israel arrived at the current conflict.

—Shoshana S. Cardin, Past Chairman,
Conference of Presidents of Major Jewish Organizations

Valuable and entertaining. It will add to the significance and enjoyment of Passover in any Jewish home.

—Michael Medved, talk show host and film critic

Acknowledgment

Doug & Debbie Jacob–y'all, Karen Hochberg, Barry Mase, Rick Magder, Rachel Laufer, Leibel Karmel, Edna Dabonka, Hollywood Bruce Kaufman, Rickaleh, Mayer and Beth Pasternak & family, Benyomin (flat tire) Nemani, Joseph Salina, Sam Glaser, Harry, Leslie, Zoe, and Peanut too, Brian, Auntie, Stella and Albert, Barry Rothenburg, Jacqlyn, and Jason, Sol, Brad Kaufman, Rabbi Guest, Eliezah, Rabbi Asher Resnick, Bootie, The Efrons, Libi's challah, Rachel Aryeh, Stanley Felsinger, Nisan & Marietta–mazel tov, Ruthee Schneiderman, Yissocher, Mrs. Kipper, Chezki, Suri, and Eliezer the pickle man, Noah Paulovic, Jon Singer, Turtle & Snail Budd.

Appreciation

Betzalel Huff, Russell & Julie Simmons & family, Dovid Winiarz, Dennis Berman, Shimon & Barry–those drycast guys, Frank Storch, Marcia Sternberg, George Rohr, Sharon Goldinger, Dootzle, E.R., Yitz, Baruch, Buck, Michael Novick, the Shabbis Malkisa Chevra, the morning Nesivos gang, Ellen Lightman, Joseph Salina, Rachel Block, Michael Schatel.

Special Thanks

Rabbi Yitzchok Lowenbraun and the Association of Jewish Outreach Professionals.

Rabbi Yigal Segal and the Jewish Literacy Foundation.

Julius Ciss. Friend, role model, and art director.

Rabbi Menachem Goldberger. A very special thanks for your hours of assistance with the manuscript. For any mistakes in this book, I take full credit.

➻ Deepest Gratitude

The Afikim Foundation

Rabbi Raphael B. Butler, a tireless visionary and source of great inspiration. Thank you for your patience.

Rabbi Noah Weinberg, *Rosh HaYeshiva Aish HaTorah*

This book is rooted in your teachings and devotion to the Jewish People. May the inspiration that readers find in these pages be a merit for your complete recovery, and many years of good health and strength.

Our Family

My parents, David & Bernice Apisdorf

Truly the greatest parents, and the greatest Bubby and Papa, anyone could ever have.

Mr. and Mrs. Robert and Charlotte Rothenburg

You will never know how much we cherish our times together. Thank you for all you do.

Baruch, Yitzie, Ditzah, Aaron, and Esther Rivka

I love you very much. Thanks for putting up with one summer's theme song: "This is the book that never ends . . . "

My wife Miriam

Every word in this book, and in the others as well, was made possible by you. Your belief, love, keen observations at so many critical junctures, and fabulous sense of humor, is woven into every line that I write, and every chapter of our life. May we continue to walk, and walk, and walk together—until 120.

Hakadosh Baruch Hu
Source of all blessing

TABLE OF CONTENTS

INTRODUCTION

Like you, I too am on a journey. And, like you, there are times when I also feel, "what a long strange trip it's been."

As Jews, there are always two dimensions to our journey—one personal and one cosmic. The personal dimension is found in the moments, days, weeks, years, people, travels, tears, joys, accomplishments, failures, and countless experiences that fill our lives. The cosmic dimension is where we are inseparable from the grand, history-spanning story of the Jewish nation. As Jews, we are part of a family with branches that reach to every corner of the planet, and roots that stretch back over three millennia.

This book is one part of my journey, and that of my family.

As a child, my parents did all they could to instill within me a strong Jewish identity, and often I did all I could do to resist. Nonetheless, thanks to them and others, I eventually *did* come to the realization that Jewish life and wisdom could be what in fact it is—the remarkably vibrant and inspiring core of my being. I feel a sense of overwhelming blessing to be able to share this slice of my journey with you; I hope that in some way yours too is enhanced.

Shana Tova

May you and all of Israel—the Jewish people—be blessed with a good, sweet, and inspiring year of life.

SECTION I

BEYOND PRAYER

PART I
THE KINGDOM

Welcome to the Main Event

If Rosh Hashanah could be summed up in one word, that word would be "king." In Hebrew, the word for "king" is *melech*. The purpose of Rosh Hashanah is that we as Jews recognize and embrace God's sovereignty—that we recognize God as *the* King par excellence. But what does this actually mean? For most of us, the notion of a king invokes images of medieval castles, Elvis, or the British royal family, and those images aren't very helpful when it comes to seeking inspiration for Rosh Hashanah. So what is a Jew supposed to do?

To embrace God as King means to understand, integrate, and commit to the ideas and ideals that are at the core of the Jewish understanding of life. So, in order to access the extraordinary potential inherent in Rosh Hashanah, we must first explore those core Jewish ideas and ideals. Then, with that understanding in hand, we will be able to unlock the door that leads, ultimately, to the King's inner chamber.

We will begin with the essential elements of the Jewish paradigm for life and then proceed to the details and see how they relate specifically to Rosh Hashanah.

Let's begin.

In a nutshell, Judaism begins with the seminal idea that God created everything that exists out of absolute nothingness and that creation has a purpose: for us to achieve the greatest meaning and pleasure possible. Anyone will tell you that if there really is a God, a "king of the universe," then being in His presence would be life's ultimate experience. This realization is at the heart of how Judaism views life: that the meaning of existence comes from being deeply connected to the sovereign source of all existence, God Himself. The way we achieve our purpose is to develop a relationship with God, and since God didn't want to leave us in the dark when it comes to developing that relationship, He gave us a manual. That manual is the Torah. The Torah is a guide for transforming every square inch of our potentially mundane lives into opportunities for connecting to God. The Torah is a detailed manual for how to infuse meaning, kindness, beauty, morality, goodness, and spirituality into every moment of our lives. In the Jewish view, every dimension of life is brimming with ultimate potential—there isn't a moment that we *can't* be in the King's Presence.

When God gave the Torah to the Jewish people, He told us that it would transform us into a "kingdom of *kohanim* (spiritual role models) and a *kadosh* (holy) nation." Within the nation of Israel, *all* the "subjects" in the kingdom are members of the royal family. The life of every Jew, and the collective life of the Jewish people, is meant to reflect the light of godliness into the world. God is our King, we have the privilege of being His emissaries, and Jewish life is the path to fulfilling that grandest and most ennobling of all human endeavors. And now, it is time for Rosh Hashanah.

Welcome to Rosh Hashanah—and Life

Rosh Hashanah takes place at the intersection of life and prayer at the dawning moments of a new year. As we will see, woven into the fabric of Rosh Hashanah are many of the keys to reinvigorating our lives in a powerful, meaningful, and even transformational way.

In the next 38 pages we are going to consider some important questions—questions like, What do we know about God? what is the fundamental nature of man? and what is life all about anyway? Then, while we are at it, we will grapple with the essence of prayer, the meaning of the shofar, the definition of spirituality, and how all of these converge to present us with the potentially life-defining moment known as Rosh Hashanah.

But First, A Note From the Author

Throughout *Beyond Survival*, you will encounter stories that appear in gray boxes. These stories are not part of the flow of the book, so if you want to skip them you can. However, if you do ignore the stories, you do so at your own peril. You see, while the book can be understood without them, they do capture a critical theme: life. Let me explain.

Throughout our prayers on Rosh Hashanah, again and again, we ask God for life: we ask to be "remembered for life" and we ask to be "inscribed in the Book of Life." When we greet one another on Rosh Hashanah we say, "May you be inscribed and sealed for life, goodness, and peace." On Rosh Hashanah God exercises His royal power of judgment and decides who will remain in the kingdom and who will not. Judgment is a very serious concept, but in a way, it is also liberating. You see, judgment implies care, concern, and love. If God didn't love us and care about each and every one of our lives, He wouldn't pay attention and bother with judgment—but He does care.

Our prayers for life are meant to be understood at face value—we want to live—but they also have a deeper meaning. Consider this: I once met a Holocaust survivor who said, "I would choose to go through all those years in Auschwitz again rather than spend one day of my life as a Nazi." That is an incredible statement, and what it means, I believe, is this: one can be alive, strong, and healthy physically yet be "dead" at the same time. A life lived in the boots of a Nazi, or under the flag of Al-Qaida or Hizbullah , is a life utterly drained of all meaning. Some choices and some actions infuse life with "life," and others drain life of everything God intended it for.

The summit of the Rosh Hashanah prayer service is the sounding of the shofar (more on that later). The Hebrew word *shofar* means "to polish or beautify." The shofar is a call to beauty—a call to morality, kindness, compassion, and sanctity. At only one place in the entire Torah are we explicitly presented with a choice: "Look closely—I have placed before you today life and good, and death and evil . . . life and death I have placed before you, blessing and curse: *Choose* life, so that you and your children will [truly] live." (Deuteronomy 30:15–19)

Ultimately, every significant choice we make is a choice between life and death. On Rosh Hashanah we not only pray to be inscribed for a year of life, we also strive to commit ourselves to living the kind of life that fills our existence with goodness, spirituality, love, and true human beauty—with life.

The stories you will encounter throughout this book are about people who made the choice to fill their lives with life. Enjoy the stories, and may we, the Jewish people, and all humankind be blessed and inscribed with a sweet year of life—a year of choosing life.

PART II
CREATION

Stop for a moment and look outside and listen. The world that surrounds us at every moment is stunning in its beauty; it is a melody, breathtaking and wondrous. Do you see? Can you hear? Allow yourself to take a moment and drink deep of the splendor and harmony that surrounds you. Can you see the ripples of perfection? Can you hear the echoes?

And yet . . .

We all know that this very same world is also a desperately dark and foreboding place. When will more towers come crashing to the ground? When and where will evil strike? Will it vanquish us all? Will it put an end to the beauty?

Life and death.

Beauty and brutality.

Light and ashen darkness.

Imagine for a moment that the future and well-being of the entire universe were in your hands. Imagine that the fate of mankind was yours, and yours alone, to shape.

Welcome to the reality called Rosh Hashanah.

Rosh Hashanah is about the universe—and each and every one of us. It's about the future of mankind—and each and every one of us. Most of all, it is about the remarkable potential in each of us to make, quite literally, a world of difference.

MEET BRAD

Josh, age six, had recently been diagnosed with a malignant tumor that had severely diminished his vision and hearing. Josh attended a camp where Brad was a music instructor. "Josh appeared dazed during our music sessions. I couldn't bear the pain of watching him in his isolated state, so I reached out to touch his hand, giving him a way to enjoy the beat the music. That moment was the beginning of a friendship that has lasted a decade." A few years later, Brad was Josh's counselor at Camp Simcha, a camp for children with cancer.

*"One evening, it was my turn to check the bunks. Chaim from Haifa was crying: he had awoken from a nightmare. I went over to his bedside and clutched his hand. 'Stay with me,' he pleaded. In a calm voice, I said '*Al Tidag *(Don't worry)* Ani Po *(I am here).' Chaim lied there holding my hand until he fell asleep. Only then did I leave to check another bunk."*

Jonathan Pollard, a Jew who spied for Israel, is serving a life sentence for a crime that usually warrants two to four years in prison. Brad has traveled to Washington three times to discuss Jonathan's plight with the staffers of seven Senators.

He has written articles and been interviewed on the radio. "It is simply not an option for me to allow the suffering of a Jew to go unanswered."

➾ *Three years after Hurricane Katrina, Brad spent a long weekend volunteering in New Orleans. "We spent hours in the scorching sun painting Janet's house. When it was time to leave, she waved goodbye as if she was sending off her dearest friends. Not only did we paint Janet's home, I think we also painted her heart."*

Brad Kaufman is a law student at the University of Baltimore.

CHOOSE LIFE

A Journey Back in Time

Let's travel back in time to the dawn of history, to the very first Rosh Hashanah. The way Judaism sees it, the world was created in seven days.* The pinnacle of creation, however, took place on the sixth day, with the fashioning of the first person. That sixth day was Rosh Hashanah. Though history began six days earlier and much was created before man, it was only with the appearance of the first person that the meaning and purpose of history began to unfold. Until the formation of

*For a scientific analysis of the Torah's understanding of time and how it relates to current physics, see Dr. Andrew Goldfinger, *Thinking About Creation*, Ch. 23-25 and. Dr. Gerald L. Schroeder, *Genesis and the Big Bang*, Ch. 27

man, the stage of history was being set, and once he existed, the curtain began to rise. We will now take a behind-the-scenes peak at what transpired as the curtain was rising.

History Begins Now

We know what the world looks like to us, but did you ever wonder what it must have looked like to the very first human being to ever set eyes on God's remarkable creation? Was it a snow-capped peak that first caught man's eye? A lush green forest? Was it the faint rumble of distant thunder or the sound of a frog splashing into a stream that drew his attention? A bird, a spider, a snowflake? What was it?

Well, guess what? The Torah tells us exactly what the world looked like the first time anyone saw it. Listen to this:

> And all the vegetation of the field had not yet appeared on the earth, and all the grasses of the field had not yet sprouted, because God had not yet caused there to be rain on the earth, and there was no man to till the soil. And a mist rose from the earth and moistened the entire surface of the ground. And then God fashioned the man, dust from the earth, and breathed into him the breath (spiritual essence) of life; and man became a vibrant personality. (Genesis 2:4–7)

In these few sentences, the Torah paints a picture of what the world looked like just minutes before the creation of man. The scene can be a bit confusing, so let's look again and consider what the words say.

First, we are told that while all the vegetation was there, it "had not yet appeared on the earth." Likewise, the grasses of the field were there, though they "had not yet sprouted." Though a mist dampened the dusty, barren ground, there was still no sign of any growth because "God had not yet caused there to be rain." At that moment, though the earth appeared to be a dead planet, it was as if every shrub and tree and flower and blade of grass was standing backstage, waiting to make some grand entrance. And this, it turns out, is exactly what our tradition teaches: God first created a world full of subterranean vegetation that was just waiting to burst forth into the light of day, but it hadn't yet rained, so the sprouting would just have to wait.

Now this seems a bit odd, don't you think? After all, couldn't God have just created a world blanketed with lush vegetation? Why all the suspense? Well, if we look at the text of the Torah through the eyes of our tradition, we discover something remarkable. It turns out that this whole seemingly convoluted way of doing things was actually meant to reveal a profound insight—an insight that goes to the very heart of what creation is all about, the purpose of our place in the world, and ultimately, what Rosh Hashanah is all about. But first, let's look again at the Torah through the lens of our tradition, and then we can try to plumb the depths of what it all means.

Of Rashi and Pixar

Rashi, the preeminent eleventh-century Torah scholar and commentator, gives us a behind-the-scenes look at how the creation of man unfolded. The following lines blend the text of the Torah with the explanation of Rashi in brackets.

> God had not yet caused there to be rain [because there was no man who was able to recognize the benefit of the rains, and] there was no man to till the soil . . . [Once man understood that the world needed it to rain, he prayed, and then it rained. Only then did all the vegetation burst forth from the ground]

> And then God fashioned the man, dust from the earth, and breathed into him the breath (spiritual essence) of life; and man became a vibrant personality. (Genesis 2:5-7)

Wow! Just imagine what the people at DreamWorks or Pixar could do with that scene. Picture this . . . the surface of the planet is a vast desolate plain. Barely a centimeter beneath the surface, a hidden world of vegetation is waiting to push through. A mist begins to rise. God gathers dust from every corner of the planet, the dust is shaped and formed into a man, and then God breathes a soul of life into this first human being. The man opens his eyes, and what does he see? Nothing—nothing but a barren landscape. Yet somehow he seems to possess an inner awareness. Somehow he senses that beneath his feet, a world of life is waiting to show itself. And he understands that all that is needed is for the rains to fall. And he understands that the key to those rains is in *his* hands, that all he needs to do is turn to God and ask for the rains and they will fall, and when they do, all the world's greenery will come rushing to the surface. Then, there will stand man, with a pristine world spread out before him, just waiting to be tilled. Pretty cool scene, no?

With this scene in our minds, let's now reflect on the first moments surrounding the creation of man, and let's ask ourselves, what does all this mean?

We now know that when God created vegetation, what He actually created was the *potential* for vegetation. After all, "it had not yet sprouted." We also know that for the barren earth to actualize its potential of becoming the lush earth, God would need to send the rains. Those rains, however, like the vegetation itself, were also suspended in cosmic pause mode. Before it could rain, God wanted to create a man capable of perceiving the need for rain—who would then ask God to bring the rain—and only then would the heavens open up and the earth give forth the fullness of its bounty.

So here's the picture . . . the world that God created was a world brimming with startling potential. The man that God created was a person capable of partnering with God in *actualizing* that potential. And do you recall what day it was that was infused with such stunning possibility? It was Rosh Hashanah. And that first person? Well, he was each and every one of us.

P-R-A-Y-E-R Spells "Man"

Now that we have a picture of what the world looked like when man was created, let's take a look at the nature of man (that's us) himself. You will recall that—

> And then God fashioned the man, dust from the earth, and breathed into him the breath (spiritual essence) of life; and man became a vibrant personality. (Genesis 2:7)

This verse captures the essence of what every human being is: on the one hand, we have a body that is formed from the "dust from the earth." In other words, we can all trace our lineage back to a common clump of dirt. For this reason, the generic Hebrew word for "man" is *adam*, which is derived from the word *adamah,* meaning "ground." At the same time, we also possess a "breath of life," a soul that emanates from God. The synthesis of these elements, the physical and the spiritual, results in the uniquely vibrant human personality.

While the standard term for "man" is *adam*, one section of the Talmud uses another word, in fact a very obscure word, as a synonym. That word, in Hebrew, is *mah'veh*. Though it is not immediately clear why this word is used, the Talmud links it to a verse in the book of Isaiah. When this verse is examined, it turns out that the word *mah'veh* actually points to a defining spiritual dimension of life.

Let's take a look at the verse. For the sake of simplicity, I have again woven the explanation of classical commentaries into the translation of the text.

> [There will come a time in history when the world will be a very, very dark place.] And the Jewish people will call to God and say, "This darkness is overwhelming." And God will reply, "You must know that even in the thick of darkness, I can bring the light in the very next moment; if you deeply desire (*mah'veh*) it, if you ask (*mah'veh*) for it, and if you correct your faults. (Isaiah 21:11-12)

For a moment, think about these verses, think about the word *mah'veh*, and then ask yourself; if the Talmud calls man a *mah'veh*, what is it saying about who we are?

It seems that the Talmud wants us to understand that we are beings capable of partnering with God in transforming even the darkest of moments into light. All we need to do is long for the light, ask for it, and do our best to be people who are deserving of the light.

When viewed through the lens of this verse, the Talmudic word for "man," *mah'veh*, means "to request" or "to pray." With the use of the word *mah'veh*, the Talmud is giving us a fascinating perspective on what makes people people. Some would say that what makes us unique is the opposable thumb or the fact that we alone reflect and ponder our place in the universe. Others would say that it's our creativity and the ability to compose baroque music, or hip-hop. With the word *mah'veh*, the Talmud asserts that what makes us unique is our ability to express our deepest desires, our deepest longings in life, through prayer.

Hmm. All this requires some review and reflection. So let's recap.

The world was created complete—almost. (Remember, no vegetation.)

Man perceived that the world was complete—almost. ("Hey, somebody forgot to take care of the landscaping.")

Man got annoyed—sort of. ("Oh, brother, this place is nothing like what the brochure showed.")

This gave rise to a desire in man—for the world to finally be completed.

This then resulted in mankind's very first act of self-expression—a request of God to finish the job already.

When trying to understand human behaviors, researchers and theorists inevitably look for root causes. Find the roots, and that will tell you an awful lot about the branches. From the vantage point of Jewish wisdom, the deepest roots of human behavior can be found in the first episode of the story of mankind.

From the outset, the first man was someone who came from exceptionally humble beginnings—the dust of the earth—and yet he possessed soaring potential. When this very first potential-filled person gazed out on the world, he was immediately bothered by the lack of completion in the world—by dissonance and disharmony. Where the world in front of him was incomplete, the first person yearned for completion, for perfection. And so he did the only thing that made any sense, he asked the Creator of the world to complete and perfect His world. And when God responded to that request—when He answered that prayer—the world became whole, and the man whose beginnings were in the dust of the earth had risen to become nothing less than God's partner in creation.

So when the Talmud chose the word *mah'veh* to define us, it was saying this: True, we may have the ability to think abstractly, reflect, introspect, and create videos for YouTube, but our uniqueness goes far beyond all that. Deep down, what makes us who we are is our ability to pray. The man (*adam*) who originated from the dust (*adamah*) is uniquely endowed with an inner yearning that enables him to become a *mah'veh*, one who prays.

But there is more.

The Perfect Vacation

In 2008, football fans everywhere held their breath as the New England Patriots made a bid for a "perfect season." Ultimately, their quest was foiled, as is the quest by millions of people for the perfect vacation, perfect marriage, or perfect job.

When you think about it, it sure seems like we are programmed for the pursuit of perfection. Something about the prospect of a perfect marriage, perfect game, or perfect work of art is almost irresistible. Perfection beckons to us, tantalizes and mesmerizes us, and urges us on in search of all that it promises. Of course, the pursuit of perfection has a serious down side. First, it's almost always illusory, and second, if we are not careful, it can become a dangerous obsession. But we are fascinated with perfection for a very deep reason. Beneath the surface, this drive is a manifestation of our deepest desire. You see, God, the Creator of the universe and the ongoing source of all existence, is pure perfection. Our drive for perfection *is* our drive for God.

In Hebrew, the word for "perfection" is *shalem*. *Shalem* means "whole, complete, and lacking nothing." The Hebrew word for "peace" is *shalom* because peace means that there is wholeness and harmony. True peace exists when all the disparate pieces in the world fit together in one harmonious, unified context.

In Jewish thought, though it is clear that we can never fully grasp what God is, one word comes as close as we can ever come to at least having some sense of God: that word is *echad*. Generally translated as "one," *echad* has a connotation that is much deeper than simply the numerical value of one. *Echad* means "pure, absolute unity." In Jewish life, the ultimate Jewish statement about *all* of reality is known as the Shema:

> *She-ma Yis-ro-el, Ado-noi Elo-heinu, Ado-noi* ***Echad***.
> Listen, O' Israel, the Lord our God, the Lord is Absolute Oneness.

The Shema is the ultimate statement about reality because the ultimate reality is perfect unity, and perfect unity is a quality unique to God. In the human realm, all perfection—and all unity—is, at best, only an approximation of ultimate unity. However, it is that very unity, that one-and-only true perfection, toward which we are all drawn. Our drive for perfection, for harmony, wholeness, and completion, is our inner drive for *Echad*, for God.

TRADITION OF KINDNESS

Shoshana Greenbaum's goal in life was to touch each of her students with her love, to enhance their self-esteem, and to help them reach their highest potential. On August 9, 2001, while visiting Israel, Shoshana was murdered by a young man who blew himself up inside the Sbarro restaurant in the heart of Jerusalem. In response to his wife's brutal murder, Shmuel Greenbaum prayed. "I prayed with great intensity to God to help me make the world better." Eventually, Shmuel launched a campaign of kindness. Today, as part of Shmuel's traditionofkindness.org, tens of thousands of people receive The Daily Dose of Kindness email.

Another victim of the Sbarro massacre was sixteen-year-old Malki Roth. Malki was a beautiful girl who was deeply devoted to caring for people with disabilities, including her severely disabled sister. In the wake of her murder, Malki's parents founded Keren Malki, a remarkable organization that "empowers the families of special-needs children to choose home care."

In July, 2008, Ofer Regev spoke at the funeral of his brother Eldad. Eldad's body had been returned to Israel in exchange for Hizbullah terrorists. He said, "We lived in a world where we believed our enemy was exactly like us. We thought we could speak to people who also wanted to raise a child, grow a flower, love a girl—exactly like us. I stand here today, sad, crying, but proud. I'm proud to belong to those who love and not those who hate."

CHOOSE LIFE

PART III

THE BIG PICTURE

To fully appreciate the awesome potential of Rosh Hashanah, we need to take a step back and look at a bigger picture. In fact, we need to look at the largest picture we possibly can. What we are going to do now is take a quick look at the ABCs of the granddaddy of all questions: What the heck is life all about anyway?

I say a "quick look" because the truth is, it would require a book to adequately deal with the subject. The following eight basic though far-from-simple ideas comprise the cornerstones of the Jewish understanding of the purpose of life. Together they form the grand context in which Rosh Hashanah, and you and I, fit. We will begin where Judaism begins, with God.

1) God, in Brief. The ability to comprehend God is way beyond us. Think of it like this: the human genome and subatomic particles like gluons and quarks are just two itty-bitty pieces of God's creation, and even they are understood by only eleven brainy professors on the whole planet. So, when it comes to comprehending what God Himself is, forget it. The best we can hope for is to grasp a bit *about* God but nothing that truly gets at the heart of what He actually *is*.

Judaism understands the nature of God's existence as absolute being. This means that God's existence does not require the existence of *anything* else—not us, not the universe, not space, and not even time. His existence is unconditional. Our existence, like everything else He created, is 100 percent dependent on God.

The notion of absolute being also includes the following: God is fully complete in and of Himself and therefore lacks and needs nothing. His existence is pure Wholeness; He is unchanging and can never become more or less in any way. Nothing exists outside Him or other than Him. He is *Echad*, absolute oneness.

2) Creation Is For Us. We know for sure that creation can't be for God's benefit because His absolute completeness means that He doesn't need anything. Creation is in no way for God and in every way for *us*, His creations. God's relationship to creation is one in which He is purely a giver. And, when God gives, He does so in a manner that is a direct expression of what He is: complete and perfect. Think about it; if you could actually have an encounter with God, would that not be the most powerful, inspiring, meaningful, and deep experience of your life?

So we are the recipients of the greatest thing, in fact the only thing that God has to offer, Himself! God created us to be the recipients of the greatest gift possible—the greatest good, the greatest meaning, the greatest pleasure, the greatest reality—Him.

3) The Yearning for Something More. Have you ever sat at the seashore, as the waves gently lapped at the sandy beach, and watched the sun dip below the horizon and the stars begin to fill the sky? Do you remember that stirring deep inside yourself? Do you remember asking yourself, "What's it all about?" Deep down we are all restless, we all long for something more. There at the seashore we sense that while we seem so small, something infinitely greater and deeper is out there, something that transcends everything else.

> Truly, self-transcendence is the essence of human existence.
> —Viktor E. Frankl, *Man's Search for Ultimate Meaning*

We feel so very, very limited, and yet we ache and yearn to merge with something larger than ourselves: with the love for another, with humanity, with the universe, and with even more—with *everything*.

Our very limitedness is the source of our deepest yearnings, and God's wholeness is the object of our deepest desires. When we search to merge with a larger reality, we are searching for God—the one and only ultimate reality. Everything that God created is, just like us, lacking. Only God is whole and complete. Only God is *One*, only God is *Echad*. Everything our souls long for is, in essence, a path, and all these paths lead to *Echad*, to God.

4) From Lacking to Complete to Prayer. The world in which we have been placed, like us, is incomplete. At best, the world is unfinished and in need of repair; at worst, it is a desolate, dark, and dangerous wasteland. Prayer begins at the horizon between the incomplete and the whole. Prayer begins with the recognition that we, like the world, are limited and lacking and that we, like the world, are in desperate need of completion and wholeness. Prayer lives in every moment where we face God—the only reality and the only wholeness—and ask to connect and relate to His *Oneness*.

5) Feeling Spiritual? The definition of "spirituality" is to be engaged in a relationship with God. The definition of a "spiritual life" is one that is guided by the desire, drive, and will to deepen that relationship and draw ever closer to God. In Jewish life, the dynamic involvement in this spiritual relationship is called *daas*.

If anybody was ever into spirituality, it was Moses, and Moses was always in search of *daas*. At one point, Moses asked God, "Please show me Your honor." Maimonides, one of the greatest scholars and philosophers of the last thousand years, explained Moses's request as follows:

> He wanted to know (*daas*) the reality of God's existence such that it would be clearly known (*daas*) in his heart . . . to such an extent that he would be aware of (*daas*) God's reality similar to the way one recognizes different people's independent realities. (Maimonides, *Foundations of Torah* 1:10)

One of the great Chassidic leaders of the twentieth century, Rabbi Shlomo Noach Berzovski wrote that—

> The entire quality of a Jew's relationship to God is dependent on how clearly enlightened his consciousness (*daas*) is in terms of recognizing his Creator . . . and the nature of this conscious awareness (*daas*) is that it infuses both one's intellect and emotions so thoroughly that he is always keenly aware of the ever-present reality of God. (*Nesivos Shalom*, Path of Daas, 11–13)

The Hebrew word *daas* means "knowledge," though its deeper meaning is "intimate connection." In life, the less we know people, the more foreign they are and the more superficial the relationship. The more we know someone, the more we can relate and the closer we can become. The fruits of spiritual living are expanded *daas*, expanded consciousness, and the harvest of a spiritual life is that we become infused with *daas* and move closer to completion, to a profound connection to God.

6) To Relate or Not to Relate? The Choice Is Yours. God never forces us to have a relationship with Him. He doesn't impose the intimacy of *daas*. Why is that so? Because, as we all know, a forced relationship is no relationship at all. For a relationship to be genuine, for it to be rich and vibrant and intimate, it must be freely chosen. And so, while God completed everything else in creation, the one thing He left undone was our relationship. That is ours to long for, ours to choose, ours to create, and ours to *ask* for. This very choosing of the relationship is the essence of prayer: "God, I want to be close to You. That is all I really want, and everything I ever ask of you is only so that we can be closer."

7) One God Seeks Partner: Must Know How to Pray and Bake. When God first put man in a position to pray for the world, He was giving man the opportunity to choose to turn to God and to fix the world. Prayer by definition is the recognition that actualization of our potential can be achieved only in relationship with God. With this in mind, let's take a look at what happened with the first person immediately *after* he prayed.

> God planted a garden in Eden, to the east, and placed the man who He had formed there . . . And God took the man and

> placed him in the Garden of Eden **to work it** and **to guard it**. (Genesis 2:8–15)

The fact that God left room for us to play a role in the completion of the world says that He wants us to be partners in creation. This active involvement attests to our awesome potential and enormous responsibility. Our partnership is rooted in prayer and then extends to the realm of action, "to work" and "to guard." Two millennia ago, the Romans had a hard time accepting this Jewish perspective on life. Let's listen in on a fascinating conversation between Rabbi Akiva, one of the greatest sages in all of Jewish history, and the Roman emperor Turnus Rufus:

> "Whose deeds are superior," the emperor asked, "those of God or those of people?" Rabbi Akiva answered, "The deeds of people are superior." Turnus Rufus then challenged him, "Look at the heaven and the earth. Can you make anything more beautiful than them?"
>
> Rabbi Akiva responded, "Do not tell me about something that is beyond human capabilities . . ." He then brought Turnus Rufus two items: stalks of wheat and baked rolls. Rabbi Akiva said, "The stalks of wheat are the deeds of God, and the baked rolls are the deeds of humans. Are these baked rolls not more beautiful?" (*Medrash Tanchuma*, Trumah)

Rabbi Akiva's point was that while people can never create stalks of wheat, *only* people can transform wheat into bread. And, the world God created was intended to be one that included not only bread, bagels and baguettes, but people of refined character, people of integrity and people reaching out to help other people.

The purpose of prayer, and the purpose of all human actions, is to partner with God in putting the finishing touches on the greatest work of art ever—creation. In drawing close to God, we not only complete ourselves, we also complete the world.

HIS FACE LIGHTS UP

➻ *Every time George sees Leah, his face lights up. Their conversations are never longer than a few sentences and often George will say something like, "I just ate, but I got a friend on the next block, maybe give it to him." George is homeless and Leah regularly prepares Shabbat leftovers for "the men" downtown. She and her siblings drive to familiar spots, see familiar faces, hand out bags of food, and then drive to the next block.*

This all started one night after Leah's family asked a waiter to pack up their leftovers. After leaving the restaurant, they went downtown for a walk by the river. There, they saw a homeless man sleeping behind some bushes. "We have that food in the car," Leah's mom said. The rest is history.

➻ *And in Houston . . .*

In the wake of Hurricane Katrina, a homeless man walked into a relief center. "I'm homeless," he said, "But I'm ready to help." A volunteer asked what he would like do. "Anything I can. I may be homeless, but there's always someone in worse shape. I may not have a home, but I have a heart."

CHOOSE LIFE

8) Call Me Prayer. Remember how we discovered that the Talmudic word for "man" is *mah'veh*, "one who prays"? Well, the Talmud itself elaborates on that concept and asks rhetorically: "And what is it that *is* the soul of a person? It is prayer." And once again, the great sage Rashi rounds out our understanding with this comment: "And the soul *is* the person's will." So *will* is the essence of who we are.

The Hebrew word for "will" is *ratzon*, and in Jewish thought *ratzon* means "that which a person's soul longs for because he recognizes that it is good." But, you might ask, we are not only souls, we are also physical beings with bodies, and don't our bodies have interests of their own? The Jewish answer to your question is, true, we do have physical interests (like lunch or a back scratch), but those interests don't well up from the core of our being the way *ratzon*-will does.

> A desire, or an interest (*chefetz*) emanates from the body. It is something that I am drawn to because of the physical pleasure to be derived, or the benefit that will result. However, will (*ratzon*) emanates from the thoughtful recognition that something is intrinsically good.
>
> —Psalms 51:18, commentary of the Malbim,
> 19th century rabbinic scholar and philosopher

Each of us is a blend of body and soul, physical and spiritual. Our bodies desire comfort, mouth-watering delicacies, and lazy days at the beach, but our souls possess a deeper *will*—the will to do what is right and good, to be connected to what's meaningful and transcendent, even if it's not what happens to be the most comfortable or delicious option in front of us. The interplay between what our souls *want* us to do and what our bodies *feel* like doing is where the freedom to choose lies. We have the ability to *will* ourselves to respond to the higher calling of our souls, despite the whining objections of our bodies.

The equation that captures these concepts is this:

If soul = prayer and soul = will, then prayer = will.

If will = our inner longing to do what's good and to connect with God, then:

prayer = the conscious focusing of one's *will* on God.

At times, we all feel conflicted—we just aren't sure who the real "me" is: "Am I a person who wants to do good, strive for spiritual living, be devoted to a meaningful cause, connect with God, or am I a person who would rather sit by the pool with a beer and soak up some rays?"

King David once said, "I am prayer." (Psalms 109:4)

The answer to the question "Will the real Shimon please stand up?" is that the "real" me is my *will*, my longing for something deeper in life, for completion. And the first and deepest expression of that real me is prayer. In Jewish law, our prayers are supposed to be audible to our own ears. Why is that? Why can't we just say prayers silently to God? The reason is *will*. Prayer is the revelation of our will, the inner yearnings of our soul, to both God and ourselves. Ultimately, what I do and what I become—what I make of my life—begins with what I want, with what I long for deep down. The road to completion begins with *will*.

PART IV

ROSH HASHANAH

This Time, It's Your Turn

Every Fourth of July my wife and I take our family to Baltimore's Inner Harbor, stake out our favorite spot for the afternoon, have a picnic dinner, and wait for the evening's fireworks. It's a lot of fun. The Fourth is a day for barbecues, fireworks, and even to think a bit about how fortunate we are to be Americans. Jewish holidays, while they may also seem to be tradition-spiced commemorations of significant historical events, are in fact something altogether different. In Judaism, holidays are far more than days when we look back at our past; rather, they are days when we literally rendezvous with our past.

The Hebrew word that the Torah uses for "holiday" is *moed*, and *moed* means "rendezvous." Every *moed,* every Jewish holiday, is a meeting of sorts. In fact, Jewish holidays are multidimensional meetings. Think of a business meeting. Imagine that you have plans to meet with someone at 2:30 p.m. on July 24 at your seventh-floor office on the corner of

Twelfth and Main. Is this not a multidimensional meeting? It is taking place within the dimensions of space, as indicated by the location of your office, the dimension of time, as indicated by the date and hour of the meeting, and most importantly, within the human dimension. In a sense, this is what *moed* is all about.

Jewish holidays are rendezvous that incorporate not only the dimensions of time and place but spiritual dimensions that go to the heart of what it means to be a Jew. To appreciate the depth of these holiday-*moed* events, we need to first look at some of the primary components that converge to form the experiential framework of these extraordinary days. Let's take a look.

Rendezvous With Whom?

Whom do we rendezvous with? Well, with God, who else?

You will recall that the most seminal idea shaping how Jews relate to God in general and the holidays in particular is that since God is complete and lacks nothing, creation can't possibly be for the Creator; rather, it is for *us*. And since, when God does things He does them right, Judaism understands that the purpose of our existence is that we enjoy being able to partake of the absolute best God has to offer. Just what is this absolute best? It's the Creator Himself, and the way we partake in the purpose of our creation is to be engaged in a relationship with God. It is with this perspective that we can gain a comprehensive understanding of the Jewish holidays—Rosh Hashanah in particular.

Every Jewish holiday is a *moed*, a rendezvous, and every Jewish holiday represents a different dimension of our relationship with God. In Jewish life, we don't just recall historical events, and we don't even reenact them; rather, we re-engage them.

> With every historical event that causes a great spiritual light to shine, [like the Exodus from Egypt] Creation is moved closer to its rectification and completion. Each year, when the date of that event returns, that same quality of spiritual light shines again and is accessible to those who connect to it.
>
> —Rabbi Moshe Chaim Luzzato, *The Way of God*, 4:7:6

> Holidays are not just historical anniversaries, rather they are times when we return and gain access to the original spiritual essence of what took place.
>
> —Rabbi Eliyahu Dessler, *Letters from Eliyahu*, Vol. 2:21

Every Jewish holiday is a portal of spiritual energy that enables us to once again tap into the deepest essence of what originally took place on that day. On Passover we re-engage the spiritual power of liberation; on Chanukah we again encounter the power of light. Though the events that took place are long gone, the way in which those events shape and nurture our connection to God are eternal. With each holiday, as we again access a rich inner world, we reach for a fresh opportunity to deepen our relationship with God—which brings us to Rosh Hashanah.

Rosh Hashanah, the Universe, and a Tuning Fork

According to the mystical teachings of Kabbalah, two principles inherent in our nature, when taken together, expand the reaches of our potential beyond almost anything we can imagine. The first of these is the man-as-micro-universe principle. The second is the man-as-tuning-fork principle.

The first principle says the following: God didn't create just one world; He actually created two. World number one is the vast universe we inhabit, from every particle in every atom to every light-emitting photon shining from every star in the sky. World number two is each of us.

The Hebrew word for "world" is *olam*. The vast universe is referred to as *olam ha'gadol*, the great macro-universe. The human being is referred to as *olam ha'katan*, the small micro-universe. The word *olam* itself actually has a dual meaning: it also means "concealment." If you have ever sensed that within you stirs a world of potential, you're right. Within each of us lies a universe of hidden potential.

HOUSE OF HOPE—AND POTENTIAL

Steve is a recovering alcoholic. As a teenager, even while he was the popular star of his high school basketball team, he was already well on his way to addiction. Later, after dropping out of college, he was one step away from spending his nights on the streets of downtown Baltimore. Eventually, Steve found his way to the front door of House of Hope, a group home for Jewish addicts and alcoholics. At House of Hope, Steve found people who believed in his potential. Today, two years after his graduation from law school, Steve is a practicing attorney who does pro bono work for other recovering alcoholics.

House of Hope was started by Jon and Ida Singer, two people with no prior experience in dealing with addicts.

According to Jon,

I met a fellow who had turned to the Jewish community for help with his drug-addicted son. The community had nothing to offer and his son ended up dying from an overdose. When I heard that story, I knew I had to do something. I owned an abandoned house in a bad neighborhood that I was on the verge of selling. Instead, I decided to renovate the house. I raised the funds, hired a small staff, and my wife did a lot of the cooking. On Friday nights we made a Shabbat dinner for the guys, on Passover we had a Seder, and on Chanukah we lit the menorah. Mostly, we tried to show the guys that we believed in them.

You know, every year we go to synagogue and ask God to remember us. Well how in the heck can we stand there and ask God to remember us if we forget about our fellow Jews? I mean, come on! These kids are like onions. They may not smell too good on the outside, but when you peel back the layers, there is something beautiful inside every one of them. A lot of them aren't going to make it. I know, I've been a pallbearer at too many funerals of guys who just couldn't beat the disease. We don't know who will live and who will die—that's God's territory—we just have to do the best we can with everybody, no matter who they are.

These days, Jon is no longer involved in House of Hope, though it's not unusual for the Singers to have the occasional recovering addict staying in their home. In addition to running his business, doting over his grandchildren, and mentoring young entrepreneurs, once a month, Jon drives over an hour to visit Jewish inmates at the Maryland Correctional Institute. He has been making that monthly trek for twenty-five years.

A recent call to the Singer home says it all.

"Hi Jon. It's Steve. This is kind of embarrassing, but my mother wants to speak with you."

"Mr. Singer," she says, "today is Mother's Day, and if it wasn't for you, I wouldn't have a son to spend the day with. Thank you."

Jon assured her that "Steve is the one who did all the hard work. It's really him we should thank."

CHOOSE LIFE

This is the entirety of what a person is; every particular strength, capacity and ability in a person corresponds to a force in the universe. In essence, they are mirror images of one another.

—Rabbi Chaim Volozhin, leading 19th century scholar, kabbalist and founder of the modern yeshiva movement. *Nefesh Hachaim* 1:6

With the man-as-micro-universe principle in mind, let's now look at the man-as-tuning-fork principle. It works like this: a tuning fork is designed so that when it is struck it vibrates, emits a musical note, and sends out sound waves at a certain pitch. Tuning forks can be calibrated to different musical notes. If you strike a tuning fork and another tuning fork happens to be nearby and is calibrated to the same note, then the second one will begin to hum the same tune as the first. (If you are really lucky, it might even do a little dance.)

The kabbalistic teachings that plumb the depths of the hidden, spiritual workings of the universe—and life—teach us that our relationship to the universe is similar to that of one tuning fork to another. We all know that our choices and actions have a dramatic effect on our lives; the man-as-tuning-fork principle says that our actions also have far-reaching, though often unseen, consequences on a much larger scale than just our personal lives.

> God designed creation in such a way that man's free willed actions have a direct impact on the transcendental forces that are the inner workings of the universe. This is true not only of actions but even words and thoughts . . .
>
> —Rabbi Moshe Chaim Luzzato,
> 18th century kabbalist, *The Way of God* 1:5

Together, these two principles place near-limitless potential in our hands. Each of us is unique—a unique universe—and with God as our partner, there is no telling how much this great potential can achieve. The unfolding story of all this great potential begins on Rosh Hashanah, the anniversary of the creation of man.

Rosh Hashanah: The One and Only You

We are now ready to zoom in for a closer look at Rosh Hashanah and ourselves.

Listen to this.

> From the time the world was created, no two days and no two people are alike. Every individual has an absolutely unique role to play in history, and no person can achieve in this world what someone else was created to achieve.
>
> —Rabbi Isaac Luria (the Ari), 16th century master kabbalist

There is nothing quite like watching my ten-year-old son take the pitcher's mound for a Little League playoff game. For me, it's like the whole world comes to a halt: one gutsy kid, one moment frozen in time, and one game that is unlike any other that has ever been played—ever. That's kind of what it was like when Adam was created. It was just him and the world: one man, one moment, and one unique set of circumstances that would never again be replicated—ever.

Just like Adam and his moment were unique, each of us is absolutely unique. Every day, in fact throughout the day, the confluence of person, place, circumstance, presence of others, and moment in history presents us with a series of moments unlike any other in all of human history. At each of those moments, it's up to us, and us alone, to reach down, pick up the ball, and do our very best to throw a strike. This reality is particularly true on Rosh Hashanah.

Rosh Hashanah puts us in Adam's shoes (which were probably something like Birkenstock sandals). When Rosh Hashanah comes, each of us is standing in the shoes of the very first person in the world. For each of us, not only is Rosh Hashanah the dawn of a new year, it's the dawn of history. For each of us, a world of potential is at our fingertips, pleading for our attention—begging for actualization.

Looking again at the account in the Torah of the creation of the first people, we find a very peculiar statement.

> Let us make man. (Genesis 1:26)

When God said "Let *us*," whom exactly was He speaking to, the plumber? The answer is that He was speaking to us, to you and I, to all of *us*.

> God therefore addressed this newly fashioned lump of clay which was to be man, and said, "Let *us* make man." You and I together will make man. I will give you the capacities and the potential and I will assist you in the process, but the work must ultimately be your own.
>
> —Rabbi Abraham J. Twerski, M.D. Founder and medical director of the Gateway Rehabilitation Center, *Let Us Make Man*

TO SDEROT WITH LOVE

On the evening of March 6, 2008, an Arab walked into the library of the Mercaz Harav Yeshiva in Jerusalem and slaughtered eight young men as they studied Torah. Seven of the victims were teenagers. The next morning, thousands of people filled the streets around the yeshiva where the bodies, each wrapped in a tallit, were brought to be eulogized. Eight families, eight worlds, all of Israel, and Jews everywhere cried out in anguish.

Reena and Nechama were in Israel for a year of post high school Jewish studies before going on to college. Like seemingly everyone else in Jerusalem, they simply had to be at the funeral. Said Reena, "To witness all that pain was overwhelming beyond anything I could ever express. It struck me, however, that beneath the pain there was strength. No one spoke of revenge. You could sense, even through the anguish, a faith in God and an air of deep holiness. All year, I had been thinking about visiting Sderot, to show them that they had not been abandoned. At the funeral, I knew the time had come. My heart told me that the way to respond to these murders was for Jews to reach out in love to one another."

After the funerals, Shabbat arrived in Jerusalem. Sunday morning, at 6:00 am, Reena and her friend Nechama went to a grocery store where they purchased ten bags of flour and everything else they needed. After three hours of baking, they had 400 chocolate chip cookies. Said Nechama, "We took cookie pans, sandwich bags and blue ribbon with us on the bus. By the time we reached Sderot, we had a hundred bags of cookies ready to go." Nechama knew a family in Sderot and a woman named Tali met them and drove them to a neighborhood where a lot of young families live. "In Sderot, people live under constant threat of missile attacks from Gaza. At any moment, the "Red Alert" can sound and from that point you have fifteen seconds to take cover. Tali had a recording of the Red Alert alarm on her phone and played it for us so we would recognize it if it sounded."

Reena and Nechama went to a park where they saw five mothers sitting and watching their children play. The mothers were thrilled to have

> *visitors and the children were overjoyed with their fresh baked cookies. A six-year-old girl, Moriah, adopted the two of them and took them all around the neighborhood. "We went from apartment to apartment," Reena said, "and for over four hours Moriah never let go of my hand—she was so sweet. They were all so sweet, and so happy to see us. At every apartment we were invited in for lunch. Had we accepted those invitations, we could have spent a week in Sderot." Over the next few months, Reena went back to Sderot where she spent Shabbat with Moriah's family.*
>
> CHOOSE LIFE

On Rosh Hashanah, God is inviting us back to the threshold of our own personal history. The script is ours to write. The choices are ours to make. The path is ours to blaze, and it all begins with turning our attention to God. We look at ourselves, our lives, and the world with the understanding that things need to be much more whole—much more beautiful—and we ask Him to make it rain. We ask Him to allow us to be His partner in creation, His partner in the *completion* of creation.

So, like the very first human being, we begin our year—our journey—with a prayer. But that's not where it ends. Prayer is the necessary first step; it's the prerequisite to everything else, but it's not *all* there is.

The Shema, the Shofar and Beauty

> If Nature is so beautiful, why should the theories that describe it not be so too? The French mathematician Henri Poincare stated: "Nature is beautiful. If Nature were not beautiful, it would not be worth studying, and life would not be worth living." A theory is beautiful when it has an air of inevitability . . . Inevitable, simple, congruent with the whole: Those are the hallmarks of a beautiful theory. It is, in fact, this aesthetic yearning for congruity with the whole that has spurred on physicists of the last two centuries to search for a Theory of Everything that could encompass all physical phenomena in the universe and unify the four fundamental forces of nature.
>
> —Trinh Xuan Thuan, *Chaos and Harmony: Perspectives on Scientific Revolutions of the Twentieth Century*

Rosh Hashanah is a day filled with prayer, with reflection on our potential, with thoughts about those we love, and with high hopes and good wishes for a sweet year. There is also a specific mitzvah, a commandment, that God has instructed us to carry out on Rosh Hashanah—the mitzvah of Shofar.

> There is a commandment in the Torah to hear the sound of the shofar on Rosh Hashanah.
>
> —Maimonides, *Laws of the shofar*

On Rosh Hashanah, every Jew is obligated to hear (*shema*) the "voice" of the shofar. While just one person needs to blow the shofar, we are all commanded to *hear* what it has to say. The sounding of the shofar, and our listening, takes place in the midst of the prayer service. The two go hand in hand. The Hebrew word *shofar* literally means to "beautify" or to "polish." What we hear in the sounding of the shofar is a voice that beckons us to beauty, a voice that asks us to polish ourselves and bring out a deep, rich inner beauty.

Remember the Shema and *echad*?

- Shema: Listen, O' Israel, the Lord our God, the Lord is absolute oneness (*Echad*).
- *Echad*: Complete, whole, harmonious beauty.

At its deepest, science is the search for the underlying beauty that ties the universe together in one simple, harmonious theory. Jewish life, at its deepest, is a finely designed instrument for drawing out that ultimate underlying beauty and making it manifest in ourselves, others, and the world around us.

When we listen (*shema*) to the shofar's call to beauty, we are hearing the echoes of the Shema, the harmonious *echad* that calls out to each and every one of us. As we will see, the core text of the Rosh Hashanah prayers paint a picture of what a truly beautiful world would look like. Our response to the call of the shofar is to pray for that world and to commit to moving ourselves, and the world, closer to the magnificence God created us for.

A RAISE IN SALARY

Chaim had good news for his wife Sarah; his boss had finally given him a raise in pay. Chaim and Sarah lived with their large family in Jerusalem in the 1940's. They struggled to make ends meet and more than once, their children went to sleep with less than full stomachs. They thanked God that now they could do more for their children.

Elsewhere in Jerusalem . . .

The Stein's barely had enough to eat from day to day. On Shabbat, though their Friday night dinner was filled with beautiful singing, their dinner plates had very little to offer. Fortunately, the owner of a small grocery store launched a "promotional campaign" and started sending them regular deliveries of food. They thanked God for this unexpected blessing.

Also in Jerusalem . . .

Rabbi Yosef B. Rubin was trying to think of how to help a poor family in a way that they would never know where the help came from. His idea for helping Chaim and Sarah, and the Steins', worked perfectly. Eventually he thought of another idea. Rabbi Rubin thanked God for the idea.

Until his death in 1977, Rabbi Yosef B. Rubin single-handedly supported hundreds of poor Jerusalem families with anonymous gifts. Today, Od Yosef Chai, the organization founded by Rabbi Rubin's son-in-law, supports thousands of poor families in Israel and America.

CHOOSE LIFE

In Partnership with God

God created the first man—and each of us—to be His partner. This is how the partnership works: each of us is a world unto ourselves as well as a microcosm of the universe. By our choices and actions, we shape our lives, impact others, and have a cosmic influence on the direction and well-being of all creation. God, for his part, is the great majestic conductor of the symphony of creation.

At any given moment, God orchestrates circumstances that are finely crafted to give us an opportunity to do something that makes a genuine difference in terms of both the *olam ha'gadol*, the macro-universe, and the *olam ha'katan*, our personal micro-universe. Both the universe and I are incomplete and in search of harmony, beauty, and wholeness. As I live in a way that draws out, refines, and polishes the wholeness of my own private world, that very endeavor reverberates and makes a unique contribution to the emerging wholeness of the world at large.

God does with me exactly what He did with the very first person: He puts me in the perfect position to succeed. A world brimming with potential, a world aching for the emergence of exquisite, breathtaking completion, was the world into which man first stepped. The first man sensed the presence of all that potential and himself longed for completion—as do we. On Rosh Hashanah, we stand as individual worlds in search of completion, we look out at a much bigger world also in search of completion, and we are confronted with a choice: Will I embrace the beauty inherent in my potential, long for it, choose it, and move myself and the universe closer to wholeness, or will I move us further away?

And now, it's time for prayer.

So let's go, because Rosh Hashanah, life, and all of creation are waiting for us.

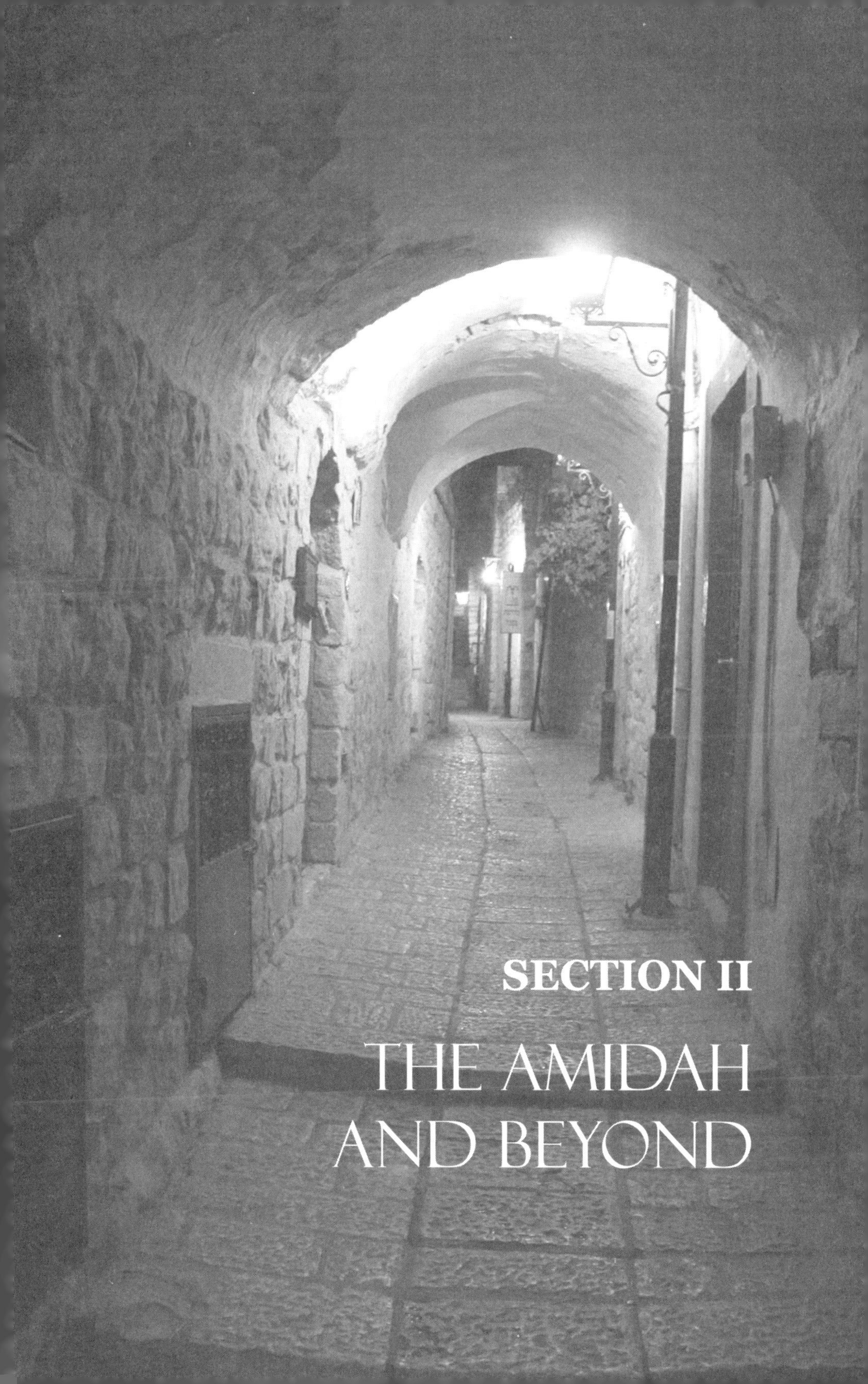

SECTION II

THE AMIDAH AND BEYOND

PART I

THE SPIRITUAL HISTORY OF THE AMIDAH

The Amidah touches the spiritual core of the Jewish people, and of every Jew. The only way to fully appreciate the meaning of the Amidah, is to understand its place in the context of Jewish life and history. So that is where we will begin, with an overview of the essence of Jewish history.

From Sinai to the Amidah

All of Jewish life, and all of Jewish wisdom, is part of a vibrant, spiritual tradition that has been handed down, generation after generation, from parent to child, and from teacher to disciple. As a Jew, you are part of a chain that stretches back over 3,000 years. Throughout the last two millennia, wherever Jews have been (and we sure have been in a lot of places), there have always been three primary texts that have been at the heart of Jewish living: the Torah (Five Books of Moses), the Talmud (the oral elucidation of the commandments and

From Adam, to the Amidah, to You: A Concise Timeline

Adam, the first human being, utters the first prayer	1
Abraham journeys to Israel and prays in Jerusalem	2147 / 1738 B.C.E.
Exodus from Egypt; Torah given at Mount Sinai	2448 / 1312 B.C.E.
First Temple built in Jerusalem; King Solomon	2935/ 825 B.C.E.
First Temple destroyed; Babylonian and Persian exile	3338 / 423 B.C.E.
Great Assembly of Sages begins the Amidah text	3351 / 410 B.C.E.
Second Temple built in Jerusalem	3408 / 352 B.C.E.
Second Temple destroyed by Romans	3830 / 70 C.E.
Great Assembly of Sages completes the Amidah	3960 / 200 C.E.
Jews in Baghdad and Prague pray with the Amidah	4560 / 800 C.E.
Jews in Germany and Aleppo pray with the Amidah	5060 / 1300 C.E.
Jews in Madrid and Poland pray with the Amidah	5460 / 1700 C.E.
You, and Jews around the world, pray with the Amidah	Today

laws in the Torah), and the *siddur*, the prayer book. Each of these texts has its own history.

The words of the Torah were spoken by God to Moses and the Jewish people on Mount Sinai. Moses himself wrote the first Torah scrolls. Since that time, highly trained and dedicated scribes have been writing Torah scrolls—letter for letter, and word for word—just like the one first written by Moses. The Torah that Moses wrote, and the Torah scroll in your synagogue, are the same Torah. The Torah contains all the commandments, laws, insights, moral principles, wisdom, and spiritual teachings necessary for every Jew, as well as the Jewish nation, to fulfill its potential. The five books of the Torah, however, only present all of these matters in broad, general terms. The Torah is the big picture of Jewish life, the details are found elsewhere.

On Sinai, God also gave Moses the details of the Torah. For a thousand years, the myriad details and applications of Jewish law were transmitted orally from parent to child, and from teacher to student. In every generation, the leading sages of the era were entrusted with ensuring the integrity of this transmission. That's how God intended it, and that is how the Jewish nation functioned in the land of Israel; as a dynamic, flourishing, chain of tradition, teaching, and life: never has there been anything like it in all of human history. Throughout the course of day-to-day life, this living tradition enabled Jews to live in accordance with the Torah. The tradition not only guided them in the practicalities of life, it also molded their inner lives. In those times, prayer, the deep expression of a Jew's personal relationship to God, was something that flowed spontaneously from every Jewish heart and soul. Then, 900 years after the Jewish people settled in Israel, dark clouds gathered over Jerusalem. With the arrival of expansive empires from Babylon, Persia, Greece, and Rome, the stability of life in Israel was shaken. Soon, it became apparent that the tranquility that had enabled the transmission to flow seamlessly from generation to generation would be a thing of the past. Finally, the greatest sages of Israel embarked on a mission that would be a defining event in Jewish history. They began to commit the oral traditions to writing.

The final result of this momentous undertaking to preserve the panoramic richness of Jewish life, even in an era of upheaval and exile, was two great texts: the Talmud, and the Amidah. The Talmud contains all of the details that had once remained oral, as well as the principles that allow Jewish life and law to respond to new conditions in ways that are in harmony with the Torah—with God's Will for the Jewish people. The Amidah, and eventually the prayer book that was composed around it, contains all of the spiritual touchstones that would forever nurture the inner life of the Jew as he or she strove to connect to God. In a sense, the Talmud guaranteed the survival and vibrancy of how Jews lived, while the Amidah guaranteed that Jewish life would always have a deep, inner spirit. Today, and every day, that Amidah is yours.

> With the writing of the Talmud, our wise men, and the Assembly of Great Sages, enabled the laws of the Torah to live forever. Similarly, with their authorship of the prayers, these sages enabled the deep, inner wisdom of the Torah to live forever.
>
> —Rabbi Shlomo Twerski, *Malchut Shlomo*

The Soul of the Hebrew Language

Before we take a closer look at the Amidah, we will need to take a slight detour into the world of the Hebrew language. Follow me.

Carpenters build with hammers and nails; artists use paints, brushes, and canvas: did you ever wonder what God used when He created the world? The answer is Hebrew letters and words. At its deepest, the universe is made out of information and knowledge—God's knowledge. The Kabbalah teaches that Hebrew is far more than just a language, and far more than random sounds that happen to be associated with certain objects or ideas. There are numerous dimensions of meaning in each and every letter, and each and every word. For example, every letter in Hebrew is simultaneously a word, a concept, and a number. Even the shapes of the letters are saturated with hidden meaning—and even the white spaces within the letters have meaning.

In the physical sciences, physicists have uncovered a startling sub-atomic level of reality where matter is made of particles like electrons, muons, and neutrinos. On a far deeper level, Kabbalah reveals how everything is made up of "spiritual energy" hidden within the Hebrew letters. Hebrew letters are the primordial spiritual elements that God used to fashion the universe. When we use Hebrew words in prayer, we are using a language that does far more than communicate—it resonates with our souls and with the fabric of the universe. Of course, if you don't understand Hebrew, it's perfectly fine to pray in English, though it's well worth the effort to learn a little Hebrew so you can tap into some of its awesome power.

And now, back to the Amidah.

The Soul of the Amidah

The Amidah was authored by the members of the Great Assembly of Sages. These were men of enormous spiritual stature, who played a decisive role, at a critical juncture in Jewish history. These sages were not only great scholars, but also great kabbalists who possessed a profound understanding of the inner workings of the universe, and the Jewish soul: a number of them also attained the lofty spiritual state of prophecy.

The sages, in their careful wording of the Amidah, built in multiple layers of meaning. One layer addressed the yearnings and longings of the Jewish soul. Think of it this way: The sages may not have been able to advise us on a career choice, because those kinds of matters change all the time, but other things are forever. The longing of the soul for meaning, for wisdom, for God, and for Jerusalem—these are the stuff out of which our souls are made—in every place, and in every era. In life, however, we often lose touch with our deepest selves: this is where the Amidah comes in.

The Amidah was crafted by master artisans of the spirit, and can awaken the Jewish heart to expressing its deepest desires: it can focus our soul and our will—the core of who we are—on our ultimate dreams. The sages, with their understanding of the Jewish soul, and with their mystical knowledge of how Hebrew words embody spiritual energies, composed prayers with the timeless ability to touch and inspire every Jew. The words of the Amidah are like spiritual sparks capable of igniting our deepest aspirations.

A Word of Caution

If this Rosh Hashanah is your first time saying the Amidah, you may find it to be a very powerful experience—though there are no guarantees. For some people, the Amidah resonates right away; for others it can take a while, and for others it's hit-and-miss—sometimes they feel connected and sometimes they don't. Even within the Amidah, there may be certain paragraphs or phrases that "speak to you," and others that don't. The truth is, prayer is a never-ending endeavor. At its core, the Amidah is a pathway for us to develop a personal relationship with God, and that takes time—a lifetime.

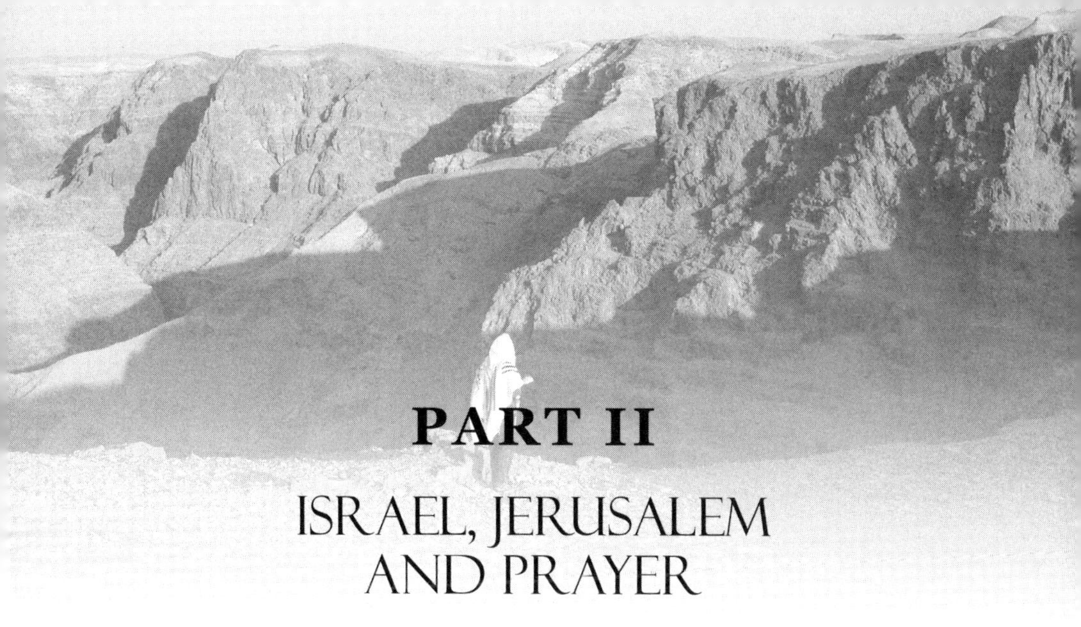

PART II

ISRAEL, JERUSALEM AND PRAYER

The photographs in this book are of the land of Israel and Jerusalem. Would you like to know why? The reason is that there is a profound connection between Israel, Jerusalem, and prayer. Allow me to explain.

Long, Long Ago

The roots of prayer run deep in Jerusalem. Thirty-six hundred years ago, Abraham prayed in Jerusalem. Four hundred years later, in the Sinai desert, God instructed the Jewish people to build the *Mishkan*, a portable sanctuary, where God's "presence" would be intensely manifest. Though constructed in the desert, the Mishkan was destined for Jerusalem. Then, twenty-eight hundred years ago, one of the greatest events in Jewish history took place—King Solomon dedicated the First Temple in Jerusalem. The Temple was the permanent structure for the Mishkan, and Jerusalem—crowned by the Temple—was both the corporeal and spiritual capital of the Jewish homeland.

During the Temple dedication ceremony, King Solomon addressed the nation. In his address, he spoke about the relationship of prayer to Israel, Jerusalem, and the Temple. This is part of what he said.

> For any prayer that any one of Your entire nation Israel may have—for each person knows what troubles his heart—when his hand reaches out [in prayer] towards this House: May You listen from heaven . . . because only You know the hearts of each person. And also the gentile . . . who will come and pray towards this House: May You listen from heaven.
>
> When Your nation goes to war . . . [or when] they are taken as captives to the enemy's land—far or near—and they will pray to You facing the land that You gave to their forefathers; facing the city that You have chosen, and facing the House that I built for Your Name. (King Solomon, Kings I 8:37-48)

In his address, King Solomon seemed quite confident that when Jews would find themselves outside of Israel, they would always pray facing Israel, Jerusalem, and the Temple. What made him so sure—did he have some sort of Jewish crystal ball? After all, God *is* everywhere. It seems that King Solomon may have studied his Torah a bit. Let's take a look at a couple of lines that blend the text of the Torah with the explanation of Rashi (an 11th century scholar and preeminent Torah commentator), in brackets. The setting for these verses is approximately 3,230 years ago. After 40 years in the desert, the Jewish nation was preparing to cross the Jordan River and enter the land of Israel. Moses had been told by God that while he had led the nation out of Egypt—across the Red Sea to Mount Sinai and through the desert—he would not be leading them into the Promised Land. Joshua was about to be handed the reins of leadership, and Moses's last days were drawing near. At that point, Moses turned to God in prayer.

> And I prayed to God at that moment, saying, "My God . . . please allow me to cross over and see the good land that is on the other side of the Jordan; this good mountain [Jerusalem], and the Lebanon [the Temple]. (Deuteronomy, 3:23-25)

Think about this: Moses had achieved so much in his life; he had been chosen by God to lead the Jewish people out of Egypt, he received the Torah on Sinai, and he achieved unparalleled closeness to God—yet he still wanted to go higher. Moses was yearning for even greater intimacy with his Creator, and this, he understood, could only be realized if he crossed the Jordan. Moses knew that only in Israel could he achieve a deeper connection to God. To go even deeper, he would need to be in Jerusalem—and to achieve the ultimate in spirituality—he would need to enter the Temple. For Moses, none of this was to be. That yearning, however, would always live in the Jewish soul. Prayer is the way we express our longing for God. As Jews, in our moments of deepest longing, nothing could be more natural than to turn towards Israel, Jerusalem, and the Temple.

Jerusalem and Rosh Hashanah

Rosh Hashanah takes place on the anniversary of the creation of man. Would you like to hear something amazing? We have an ancient tradition that says God began all of creation from a single "point"—and that point is centered on the Temple Mount, in the heart of Jerusalem. Our tradition also teaches that the first person was created on the Temple

Mount. The origins of the universe, and the origins of mankind, are rooted in Jerusalem. As we have seen (check out page 13), the very first thing that the very first person did, was to pray. It is no wonder that our forefather Jacob referred to Jerusalem as, "the gateway of heaven." (Genesis 28:17) The kabbalah teaches that no matter where one is when he or she prays, that after leaving our hearts and out lips, our prayers "travel" to Israel, Jerusalem, the Temple, and then to God.

Jerusalem, Rosh Hashanah, and You

Today is Rosh Hashanah, a day that exists at the timeless intersection of creation, Jerusalem, and prayer. Jewish law states that a person praying in Israel should always face Jerusalem, and in Jerusalem, one should face the Temple. Synagogues around the world are built facing Jerusalem. Today, when you say the Amidah, you will turn towards Jerusalem. When you do, you will be joining together with Jews around the world, and Jews throughout history.

If you have been to Jerusalem, then you know its power. You have stood beneath her enchanting sky; you have touched her Wall, and it has touched your soul. If you have been to Israel, I hope the photographs in this book will serve as touchstones that reconnect you—and your prayers—to something very, very deep. If you haven't been to Jerusalem, then I have a secret to share with you: you are connected nonetheless. From creation, to Adam, to Abraham, to Moses, until this very day—whenever we pray—we are rooted in Jerusalem.

Oh, and by the way, if you haven't been to Jerusalem: what are you waiting for?

PART III

FIFTEEN TIPS FOR A MEANINGFUL AMIDAH

Bob Dylan once walked into a synagogue and asked the stunned rabbi if he could speak for a minute from the pulpit. He then posed the following question to 600 people who were as silent as a stained-glass window. "Hey, people, how *does* it feel to be on your own, with no direction home, like a complete unknown, like a rolling stone?" With that, Dylan smiled, walked down the aisle, and out of the synagogue. Everyone began to talk. "I *do* feel like I'm on my own," a retired electrician said, "I have no idea what any of these prayers are about." "Me too," said a college freshman, "I can't make sense of any of this stuff. If anybody in this place is a rolling stone, it's me." "I know how you feel," remarked a 32-year-old pediatrician," I really could use some direction." The pediatrician's mother mumbled under her breath, "All that money on medical school, and you still don't have any direction?"

One of my goals in life is to make sure that you never feel like any of those people. The following list of suggestions will help you get more out of your prayer experience. Even if you use a different prayer book, these tips will be useful in any prayer or synagogue context. Whether you are an Amidah rookie, have been at this for a few years, or are a seasoned veteran, some of these suggestions will apply to you. And by the way, that story about Bob Dylan . . . I made it up.

The Beyond Survival Amidah

The Beyond Survival Amidah has two primary parts: the text of the prayer in English and Hebrew, as well as explanation and commentary. Each major section of the prayer text is followed by three explanatory elements: I. The Big Picture: a global theme for each section. II. Insights: further background and depth to specific words and phrases. III. Reflection: suggestions and guided meditations for creating a deeper connection to the prayer.

This Amidah can be used for study and preparation prior to Rosh Hashanah, and also for prayer on the holiday itself. If you are a cut-to-the-chase sort of person, we have provided a commentary-free Amidah beginning on page 149.

Fifteen Tips For a Meaningful Amidah

1. In Judaism, prayer is known as *avodah sheh-b'lev*—"devotion that flows from the heart." This means that if you have a heart, then you can pray. If your heart and soul have dreams, yearnings, and aspirations, then you have a prayer within you. So give it a try. Open the text of the Amidah, read some of the insights, say the words, and see what happens. You may be pleasantly surprised by what your heart has to say.

2. A tip from Yogi Berra. The legendary New York Yankee catcher and manager once said, "Ninety percent of this game is mental, and the other half is physical." Something similar could be said about the Amidah. Ninety percent of what it takes to have a meaningful Amidah, comes from study and preparation ahead of time; the other half comes from thinking about what the prayers mean as you say them, and the last half is about fully opening yourself up to the experience. So, pick any half you like, and enjoy.

3. Preparation. Before Rosh Hashanah, take some time to read the text of the Amidah along with the explanations in this book, and other books. Familiarize yourself with the basic structure and flow of the prayers, make some notes about what you want to focus on during your prayers, tuck those notes into your prayer book, and use them as personal guides on Rosh Hashanah. The flowchart at the end of this section will help you structure your preparation.

4. Don't freak out. The Amidah is not an all-or-nothing affair, and if the length seems daunting, you can divide it into bite-size portions. Try the following: each time you say the Amidah, pay close attention to one or two paragraphs. Contemplate the meaning of the words in those paragraphs, read the insights, and reflect. As for the other paragraphs, you can focus on them another time.

5. Patience young Padawan. The terms, expressions, and concepts in the Amidah are not the language of everyday conversation. One needs to develop a sensitivity to the language of prayer. It can take a long time to acquire a "taste" for what the Amidah is about—even years. Be patient.

6. You are not alone in this challenge. Don't think that you are the only person in synagogue who is struggling to have an inspiring, relevant Amidah. The Amidah is a challenge—and it should be. Prayer is about relating to God, and there is no end to deepening that connection and relationship. Regardless of how long anyone has been doing this prayer thing, it is always a challenge to connect in a deep and personal way to the words.

7. Prayer is not an Olympic event. The first person to finish the Amidah doesn't get a medal, there is no reason to try and keep pace with the person next to you, and if you happen to be the last person to finish—that's probably a good sign.

8. There is nothing "silent" about the Amidah. The Amidah is often referred to as the Silent Prayer, but in fact, the words are supposed to be audible. No, this isn't a shouting match to see who can get God's attention: you alone are supposed to hear the words of your prayers. You see, on the one hand, prayer begins in the heart and is then expressed with our lips. At the same time, when we hear what we are saying, there is a power in those words that can further stir our hearts.

9. "Recalculating." If you are a veteran, and you pray in Hebrew, you will immediately notice that the pages of this Amidah turn the "wrong way." Sorry. It's not that you are being discriminated against, it's just that we wanted to make the experience as accessible as possible for those who are more comfortable with the English flow of the text.

10. When part of the Amidah "hits home," stop and linger for a while. If a particular word, phrase, or paragraph

seems to be speaking directly to you—it probably is. Those resonant moments of connection can be your gateway into a fabulous experience: make sure you take advantage of them.

11. "The connection just isn't happening, it's that simple." If you become frustrated or bored with this whole experience, put it aside for a while. It's perfectly fine to put down your prayer book and pick up another Jewish book (once you have read this one three or four times), that might inspire you.

12. Get me outta here. Let's be honest, sometimes the formality of synagogue can be stifling. If you need to take a walk for a while to reflect, and be alone with your thoughts, that's okay—just don't get lost.

13. When all else fails—talk to God. Connecting to God is the essence of prayer. If you aren't achieving the connection today through the Amidah, then use your own words. The key is to speak from your heart. Share your deepest thoughts, hopes, dreams, fears, aspirations, requests, goals, and yearnings with God.

14. Effort alone is deeply meaningful. There is a metaphysical principle that says—sincere effort produces spiritual growth and benefit, even if you don't *feel* it. Participating in Rosh Hashanah services, trying to understand the prayers, and grappling with the language; each of these efforts is meaningful, and each, in some way, brings you closer to who you truly are, to the Jewish people, and to God.

15. Thank God for doubleheaders. When I was a kid, you could buy one ticket and see two baseball games. Well, Rosh Hashanah is sort of like God's doubleheader. If your

first Amidah isn't a winner, there is always the next one. If the first day doesn't go great, there is always the second day. And, if this Rosh Hashanah gets away from you, it's never too late to connect to God—tomorrow, next week, next month, or next year.

BLESSINGS YEAR-ROUND

אָבוֹת Forefathers
Spiritual roots

גְּבוּרוֹת Powers
Divine omnipotence

BLESSINGS UNIQUE TO ROSH HASHANAH

קְדוּשַּׁת הַשֵּׁם Sanctity of God's Name
A Perfect World

1. אַתָּה קָדוֹשׁ **Holy** *God's ultimate transcendence*
2. וּבְכֵן תֵּן פַּחְדְּךָ **Dread** *Universal awe of God*
3. וּבְכֵן תֵּן כָּבוֹד **Honor** *The Jewish mission in history*
4. וּבְכֵן צַדִּיקִים **Righteous** *A truly elevated world*
5. וְתִמְלוֹךְ **Sovereignty** *Eternal Jerusalem*
6. קָדוֹשׁ אַתָּה **Holy** *God's judgment*

ALL HOLIDAYS

קְדוּשַּׁת הַיּוֹם Sanctity of the Day
The gift of being a Jew

BLESSINGS YEAR-ROUND

עֲבוֹדָה Restoration of the Jerusalem Temple
Prayer and the Temple

הוֹדָאָה Gratitude to God
For every moment of life

שָׁלוֹם Peace
Ultimate blessing

אֱלֹהַי נְצוֹר My God . . .
Taking leave

PART IV

THE BEYOND SURVIVAL AMIDAH

The Amidah, your prayer, begins on the next page.

The word *amidah* means "to stand." We are now about to enter a space in which we are standing in the presence of our Creator. Before beginning the Amidah, we take three steps forward and enter a realm where nothing other than God fills our consciousness. Allow yourself to speak from the heart, in a quiet voice, audible only to your ears. Prior to the opening words of the Amidah, we offer a brief prayer: we focus, quiet our minds, and prepare for a journey to the inner world of the Jewish heart and soul.

(Take three steps backward, then three steps forward: now, it's just you and God.)

אֲדֹנָי שְׂפָתַי תִּפְתָּח וּפִי יַגִּיד תְּהִלָּתֶךָ.

⇝ אָבוֹת - FOREFATHERS ⇜

(When you say the word Blessed, *bend your knees; for* You, *bow at the waist; for* A-donai, *straighten up and continue your prayer while standing.)*

בָּרוּךְ אַתָּה יהוה אֱלֹהֵינוּ וֵאלֹהֵי אֲבוֹתֵינוּ, אֱלֹהֵי אַבְרָהָם, אֱלֹהֵי יִצְחָק, וֵאלֹהֵי יַעֲקֹב, הָאֵל הַגָּדוֹל הַגִּבּוֹר וְהַנּוֹרָא, אֵל עֶלְיוֹן, גּוֹמֵל חֲסָדִים טוֹבִים וְקֹנֵה הַכֹּל, וְזוֹכֵר חַסְדֵי אָבוֹת, וּמֵבִיא גוֹאֵל לִבְנֵי בְנֵיהֶם, לְמַעַן שְׁמוֹ בְּאַהֲבָה.

זָכְרֵנוּ לְחַיִּים, מֶלֶךְ חָפֵץ בַּחַיִּים, וְכָתְבֵנוּ בְּסֵפֶר הַחַיִּים, לְמַעַנְךָ אֱלֹהִים חַיִּים.

(When you say the word Blessed, *bend your knees; for* You, *bow at the waist; for* A-donai, *straighten up and continue your prayer while standing.)*

מֶלֶךְ עוֹזֵר וּמוֹשִׁיעַ וּמָגֵן. בָּרוּךְ אַתָּה יהוה, מָגֵן אַבְרָהָם.

→ *Amidah continues on page 74*

Request for assistance, even in prayer

(Take three steps backward, then three steps forward: now, it's just you and God.)

Adonai, my Master, open my lips so that my mouth will tell of Your praise.

The Amidah begins . . .

AVOT - FOREFATHERS

(When you say the word Blessed, *bend your knees; for* You, *bow at the waist; for* A-donai, *straighten up and continue your prayer while standing.)*

Blessed are You, Adonai, our God and God of our forefathers; God of Avraham, (Abraham) God of Yitzchak, (Isaac) and God of Yacov (Jacob):

The (God Who is the only true, ultimate) Power, *the* Great, *the* Mighty, and *the* Awesome—God Most High, Who bestows good, loving kindness and owns everything, and remembers the kind actions of the Forefathers, and brings a redeemer to their children's children, for the sake of His Name, out of love.

Remember us for life

Remember us for life, King Who desires life, and inscribe us into the Book of Life—for Your sake—Living God.

(When you say the word Blessed, *bend your knees; for* You, *bow at the waist; for* A-donai, *straighten up and continue your prayer while standing.)*

King, Helper and Savior and Shield. Blessed are You Adonai, Shield of Avraham, (Abraham).

➔ *Amidah continues on page 75*

THE BIG PICTURE

In 1775, Daniel Boone led a small expedition into uncharted territory. The path they blazed eventually became known as the Wilderness Trail. Within fifty years, over 200,000 people traveled along that route to Kentucky.

In 1738 B.C.E., Abraham, founding father of the Jewish nation, rejected paganism and blazed a trail in an uncharted spiritual wilderness. In time, Abraham's son and grandson, Isaac and Jacob, would blaze trails of their own. Abraham, Isaac and Jacob imprinted spiritual markers on the soul of the people that would eventually follow in their footsteps. We are that people. Each of us is seeking a life of meaning, depth, and connection to God. As Jews, we are not lonely wanderers, and our search does not need to take place in the dark. Our forefathers lit the way, and those lights still shine in our souls.

Like our predecessors, for each of us, there is a trail to blaze. A trail of goodness and kindness, a trail of integrity and strength of character, and a trail of sanctity and closeness to God. As we begin our prayer, it is with the awareness that we are doubly blessed. From our forefathers, we have inherited remarkable spiritual capabilities, and at the same time, God has given us each an opportunity to express and actualize our soul's unique potential.

INSIGHTS

בָּרוּךְ אַתָּה ה' - Blessed are You. These words are the essence of prayer and reflecting on them can transform your life. When we pray, we are speaking to God. When we say "You," we are talking directly to our Creator. Is that not truly awesome? Think about it. Can there be anything more awe- inspiring than being able to stand in the Presence of God and to speak to Him, pour out your heart to Him, confide in Him?

The Amidah begins precisely where Jewish life begins, with

the conviction that we can have a direct, personal, and intimate relationship with God. To achieve that connection, all we need to do is open our hearts and speak.

בָּרוּךְ אַתָּה ה׳ - Blessed are You. Obviously, we can't give God any blessings. The Hebrew word for "blessed," *baruch*, is related to the word *breicha*, which means a "free-flowing spring of water." God is the ever-flowing source of all existence, life, and blessing. With the words "Blessed are You," we are recognizing the reality of standing in the Presence of *all* blessing.

God gives blessing. We receive. In fact, receiving is all we can do. Our relationship to God is akin to the relationship between a great master and a humble disciple. The more clearly we grasp the reality that the master has everything to offer, and we have everything to gain, the more we will be able to receive.

אֱלֹהֵינוּ וֵאלֹהֵי אֲבוֹתֵינוּ - Our God and God of our forefathers. Sometimes life overwhelms us, and we feel like there just isn't any gas left in the tank. As Jews, we each have a reserve tank that was filled by our forefathers. Deep in our souls, we have the ability to tap into that reserve of spiritual energy, and to draw strength and inspiration where there seems to be none.

REFLECTION

As a Jew, you are never alone. If you are in synagogue with other Jews, then whether you feel it or not, you are deeply connected. Beyond that, you are linked to Jews throughout all of history. You are a descendent of Abraham, Isaac, and Jacob; Sarah, Rebecca, Rachel, and Leah. Our souls are all shoots from the same root; the same family and history: we all share the same destiny. We share a transcendent bond with one another and with our Creator—the Creator of the universe.

גְּבוּרוֹת - POWERS

אַתָּה גִּבּוֹר לְעוֹלָם אֲדֹנָי, מְחַיֵּה מֵתִים אַתָּה, רַב לְהוֹשִׁיעַ.
– מְכַלְכֵּל חַיִּים בְּחֶסֶד, מְחַיֵּה מֵתִים בְּרַחֲמִים רַבִּים, סוֹמֵךְ
נוֹפְלִים, וְרוֹפֵא חוֹלִים, וּמַתִּיר אֲסוּרִים, וּמְקַיֵּם אֱמוּנָתוֹ לִישֵׁנֵי
עָפָר. מִי כָמוֹךְ בַּעַל גְּבוּרוֹת, וּמִי דוֹמֶה לָּךְ, מֶלֶךְ מֵמִית
וּמְחַיֶּה וּמַצְמִיחַ יְשׁוּעָה.

מִי כָמוֹךְ אַב הָרַחֲמִים, זוֹכֵר יְצוּרָיו לְחַיִּים בְּרַחֲמִים.

וְנֶאֱמָן אַתָּה לְהַחֲיוֹת מֵתִים. בָּרוּךְ אַתָּה יהוה, מְחַיֵּה הַמֵּתִים.

→ *Amidah continues on page 78*

GEVUROT - POWERS

You are eternally Powerful, my Master,

You are the Reviver of the dead, completely able to save us.

The one Who Sustains the living with loving-kindness,

Reviver of the dead with Your greatly abundant mercy.

The one Who Supports those who have fallen, Who is the Healer of the sick,

Who frees the imprisoned, and upholds His faithfulness to those asleep in the dust.

Who is like You, Master of all powers, and who resembles You, a King Who causes death and restores life, and causes salvation to sprout.

WHO IS LIKE YOU?

Who is like You, merciful Father, Who mercifully remembers His creations—for life.

And You are faithful to revive the dead. Blessed are You, Adonai, Who revives the dead.

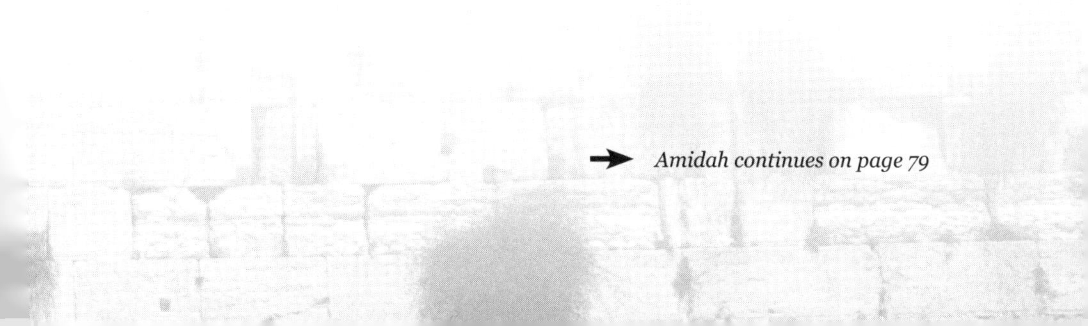

→ *Amidah continues on page 79*

THE BIG PICTURE

Do you remember that spring morning, after a night of rain, when suddenly the bare trees were budding again? Do you recall the morning when colorful blossoms appeared out of nowhere on the bushes, and when those first flowers began to open? Do you remember the first sound of the birds returning from their winter homes? Can you still smell the fragrant air—the smell of life?

Life is the greatest gift there is.

A mother who has seen her child's life saved by a lifeguard, or by a doctor, knows: life is the greatest gift there is. A son who has watched as his father's last days ebbed away, or who has seen a parent suddenly snatched away by a terrorist, knows: life is the greatest gift there is. Someone who has watched a friend take back his life from the clutches of addiction knows: life is the greatest gift there is. A woman who has given birth, and a father who has witnessed that birth, knows clearly: Life is the greatest gift there is.

God has given us all a truly priceless gift: the gift of life.

Nowhere is God's power more evident than in the gift of life.

INSIGHTS

סוֹמֵךְ נוֹפְלִים, וְרוֹפֵא חוֹלִים - Supports those who have fallen, Who is the Healer of the sick . . . The gift of life is not always easy. The gift of life also includes sickness and failure—it includes times when we feel lost and trapped. God sends disappointment, sickness, obstacles, and challenges—that is the reality. God both gives and takes life, this too is the reality—a powerful reality.

Our sages taught us, "The achievement of pleasure and sense of accomplishment in life are commensurate with the effort and the struggle."

I have a twenty-three year old friend who went through a rough bout of chemotherapy. I ran into him in the grocery store one day.

"Cancer is the best thing that ever happened to me," he said, "Now I finally appreciate the beauty of life." To be honest, I have a hard time grasping what he said, but he not only means it, he lives it.

בַּעַל גְּבוּרוֹת - Master of all powers . . . A blade of grass doesn't sway in the wind unless God enables it to sway. A cat doesn't dart across the street unless God enables it to run. Often there seems to be many forces at work in the world, yet beneath the surface there is only One. One omnipotent power that is the life force of all powers.

REFLECTION

Every minute your heart beats about 72 times. In that same minute, you take 15 breaths. In an hour, that's about 4,000 heartbeats and 900 breaths. If you were born on Rosh Hashanah in 1977, then your heart has already beat approximately 1,165,981,104 times. In that same time, you took 242,912,730 breaths—give or take a couple hundred thousand.

Let's take a moment to feel the gift of life within us. Read the next paragraph and then give it a try.

Close your eyes and take a few slow, deep breaths. Breathe at a calm, comfortable rate. Focus on your breathing, and on your heartbeat. With each breath, feel the gift of life. Every fiber in your body, and every cell, is filled with life. You are so alive. Prepare to open your eyes, but first, prepare to embrace life. Now open your eyes—to the gift of life.

קְדוּשַּׁת הַשֵּׁם - SANCTITY OF GOD'S NAME

אַתָּה קָדוֹשׁ וְשִׁמְךָ קָדוֹשׁ, וּקְדוֹשִׁים בְּכָל יוֹם יְהַלְלוּךָ סֶּלָה.

וּבְכֵן, תֵּן פַּחְדְּךָ, יהוה אֱלֹהֵינוּ, עַל כָּל מַעֲשֶׂיךָ, וְאֵימָתְךָ עַל כָּל מַה שֶּׁבָּרָאתָ. וְיִירָאוּךָ כָּל הַמַּעֲשִׂים, וְיִשְׁתַּחֲווּ לְפָנֶיךָ כָּל הַבְּרוּאִים. וְיֵעָשׂוּ כֻלָּם אֲגֻדָּה אַחַת, לַעֲשׂוֹת רְצוֹנְךָ בְּלֵבָב שָׁלֵם. כְּמוֹ שֶׁיָּדַעְנוּ, יהוה אֱלֹהֵינוּ, שֶׁהַשָּׁלְטָן לְפָנֶיךָ, עֹז בְּיָדְךָ, וּגְבוּרָה בִּימִינֶךָ, וְשִׁמְךָ נוֹרָא עַל כָּל מַה שֶּׁבָּרָאתָ.

→ *Amidah continues on page 86*

KEDUSHAT HASHEM - SANCTITY OF GOD'S NAME

You are holy and Your Name is holy, and holy ones praise You daily—forever.

AND THEREFORE, PLACE YOUR DREAD . . .

And therefore, place your dread, Adonai our God, on all Your works,

And Your awe on all You have created.

And then all Your works will fear You, and all Your created beings will prostrate themselves before You. Enable them all to form a single society, to carry out Your will with a complete heart.

For as we know, Adonai our God, that rulership is Yours alone, might is in Your hand and power is in Your right hand, and Your awe-inspiring Name is upon all You have created.

➔ *Amidah continues on page 87*

THE BIG PICTURE

Every human being is longing for something, for something more. Every human being is searching for something, for something more. Deep down, every human being is yearning for the ultimate experience of what life is all about. For decades now, Coca-Cola has been making the most audacious claim in the history of advertising. Coke claims to be "it," and to be "what you are looking for." A Coke may be thirst-quenching, but it's *not what I'm looking for*!

The most awesome, pleasurable, transcendent, and meaningful experience anyone could ever have would not be a cold coke on a hot summer day, but it would be a personal encounter with God, the source of all existence. Think about it; no matter how many powerful, inspiring, meaningful, and deep experiences you've had in life—if you could actually have an encounter with God—would that not truly be the "it" "you are looking for"?

This is the first paragraph that is specific to Rosh Hashanah and it contains a sweeping prayer for all mankind. God created all people to achieve the deepest, richest, pleasure possible—closeness to God. On Rosh Hashanah, we lift our sights as high as possible, and when we do, we discover a prayer for all humanity to recognize and relate to God, the source and essence of all reality.

INSIGHTS

קָדוֹשׁ - **Holy.** The Hebrew word for "holy" is *kadosh*. Kadosh means "something that occupies an utterly distinct and elevated plane of existence." God is "outside of" and "above" creation. His reality is unique, distinct, and beyond anything He created. At the same time, there is a miraculous potential built into the fabric of creation. Think of this potential as a spiritual ladder that can, to some degree, bridge our realm and God's realm. Wherever this bridging of worlds takes place, our world becomes elevated and invested with holiness.

The land of Israel is known as the Holy Land because it serves as a bridge between our world and God. The same is true of the Jewish people. The Torah refers to us as a "holy nation" because we too are meant to be a bridge that connects this world to the transcendent reality of God.

On Rosh Hashanah, while we recognize God as being completely "above" us, we pray that the world becomes a place of ladders reaching upwards to a higher, holier, dimension—a place where heaven and earth kiss.

פַּחְדְּךָ - Dread. Fear has a constructive role to play in our lives. We all have fears; fears of illness, of failure, and of death. While excessive fear can paralyze us, fear is natural, and healthy fear can be a powerful motivator. If life has the potential for remarkable meaning, and there is a chance we may go through life and never discover the source of meaning, *that* is something to fear. If life has an ultimate purpose, and there is a chance we may never recognize the purpose, *that* is something to fear.

If there is a God who created all of humanity for a noble and lofty purpose, and if humanity never discovered that reality, *that* would be the greatest tragedy of all. In the Jewish view of life, the greatest thing to fear is never recognizing reality.

עַל כָּל מַעֲשֶׂיךָ . . . עַל כָּל מַה שֶּׁבָּרָאתָ - On all Your works . . . all You have created. Everyone that God "created" possesses a unique and beautiful potential, but not everyone "works" to actualize his or her potential. One of the basic commitments we all need to make in life is to work with our potential in order to see that it flourishes. We do this by first asking God to help us, and then making every reasonable effort to move forward. This interplay of prayer and effort is how we strive to transform the potential we were created with into a living work of art.

REFLECTION

Can you remember a moment when you felt connected to your potential, when you felt like you were truly beginning to tap into the purpose of what your life is all about? That experience may have faded, but it doesn't have to slip away forever. Rosh Hashanah is a fresh opportunity to take hold of your potential. Go inside yourself and feel the rumblings of your potential. Reclaim it; it's yours, a unique and beautiful gift from God.

עַל כָּל מַעֲשֶׂיךָ . . . עַל כָּל מַה שֶּׁבָּרָאתָ - all Your works . . . all You have created. There is another dimension of meaning to these words. "Your works" is referring to people. "Created" is a reference to the purely spiritual beings known as angels. As purely spiritual beings, angels are never conflicted—ever. Angels never feel any tension between their agenda and God's agenda. We, on the other hand, are always conflicted. God may want us to be sensitive and kind to other people, to choose a path of integrity and spirituality in life, but the path to the couch, Blockbuster, or MySpace is much shorter and easier. You must admit, there is something attractive about the life of an angel. Life is easy if you're an angel, but their lack of conflict also means they lack the ability to make choices—ever. In that sense, angels are like fish; they just do what they are programmed to do, and that's it. You and I are different.

Our inner conflicts are the source of our inner greatness. Conflict in life is where human potential is unleashed. Every time we choose to do what's good or compassionate or meaningful—every time we try to reflect God's Will in this world—regardless of how uncomfortable, unprofitable, or unpopular it may be, we are exercising the very essence of our humanity: our ability to make moral choices.

There are a lot of creatures in God's world. Animals in the woods, fish in the sea, angels in the heavens, and people on earth. Of all God's creatures, only we can choose to be His partners in creation: only we can work to make the world a kinder place; only we can make the types of choices that can change history, and only we can make a difference.

On Rosh Hashanah we long to make positive, healthy choices in life—to choose the higher path—and we ask God to guide us in our quest.

REFLECTION

We all have an Achilles heel in life, an area where we keep making the same counter-

productive choice over and over again. As the years go by, we tend to give up. We lose hope of ever being able to make the right choice, of ever being able to be disciplined or exercise self-control, of ever overcoming our haunting inner weakness. Today, as we focus on the essence of what it means to be a Jew, we need to remember that God never, ever gives up on us. Today, all of creation is spread out before us, just like it was when the very first man and woman were created. We can always begin making the right choice—right now. We can always set a new course for ourselves despite our history—right now. We can make a choice that will change our lives forever—right now.

וְיֵעָשׂוּ כֻלָּם אֲגֻדָּה אַחַת, לַעֲשׂוֹת רְצוֹנְךָ בְּלֵבָב שָׁלֵם - Enable them all to form a single society, to carry out Your will with a complete heart. As Jews, not only do we never give up on ourselves, we never give up on humanity. Year after year, as we watch world events unfold, there is plenty of room for cynicism, bitterness, and despair. There is no end to what people can do to make the world a cold, brutal, and tortured place. Yet we pray—always—in the face of despair. We hope—always—in the face of darkness. We believe—always—in the potential for mankind to find its way to sanity—to find its way to God.

וְשִׁמְךָ נוֹרָא - And Your awe-inspiring Name . . . In Hebrew the word for "name" *shame*, has the same root as the word for "there" *sham*. "There" implies distinct identification. "There" means that you can point to something and clearly identify where and what it is. That is also the function of a name.

Have you ever had the experience where a friend was trying to describe someone else to you but couldn't recall his name? Then, as soon as they remembered his name, all the pieces fell into place. With the mention of a name, you knew exactly who the person was, distinct from anyone else in the world. In a sense, a person without a name is not completely "there." (This helps explain why the Germans stripped us of our names and gave us numbers instead.)

We long for a world of wholeness and completion. We

long for a world where people encourage one another instead of being jealous of one another; for a world of peace and not war, of love and not hatred. A world where there is not one nook or cranny where God's presence—God's "name"—isn't manifest. We long for a world where at all times and in all situations people ask only one question: "What does God want of me at this moment?" In such a world, God will be "there" and "there" and "there." His name will be everywhere.

NOW I START MY LIFE ANEW . . .

"I felt a kind of searing pain that I wouldn't wish on anyone. I saw that my leg had been hurt and the lower half seemed to be gone. I tried to crawl out of the tank and got as far as the turret when another missile exploded."

Sergeant Ohr Bar-On, age 20, lost both his legs during the Second Lebanon War.

"It was my dream since I was a boy to be a soccer player . . . Now I start my life anew, because it was given to me as a gift. I won't take anything for granted."

CHOOSE LIFE

וּבְכֵן, תֵּן כָּבוֹד, יהוה, לְעַמֶּךָ, תְּהִלָּה לִירֵאֶיךָ, וְתִקְוָה טוֹבָה לְדוֹרְשֶׁיךָ, וּפִתְחוֹן פֶּה לַמְיַחֲלִים לָךְ, שִׂמְחָה לְאַרְצֶךָ, וְשָׂשׂוֹן לְעִירֶךָ, וּצְמִיחַת קֶרֶן לְדָוִד עַבְדֶּךָ, וַעֲרִיכַת נֵר לְבֶן יִשַׁי מְשִׁיחֶךָ, בִּמְהֵרָה בְיָמֵינוּ.

→ *Amidah continues on page 96*

And also, then, grant honor . . .

And also, then, grant honor, Adonai, to Your nation, praise to those who fear You, and good hope to those who are searching for You, and an open mouth to those who yearn for You:

Joy to Your land and rejoicing to Your city; a proud, sprouting shoot to David Your servant, and a prepared light for the son of Yishai (Jesse), Your anointed, speedily in our days.

→ *Amidah continues on page 97*

THE BIG PICTURE

Has there been a people in history less honored than the Jewish people? How many nations have been saddled with the collective guilt of murdering God? Only one, the Jewish nation. How many nations have been accused of manipulating world events for their own nefarious ends? Only one, the Jewish nation. How many nations have been forcibly expelled from England, France, Spain, Italy, Iraq, Tunisia, Syria, Egypt, and Morocco? Only one, the Jewish nation. How many United Nations member states are barred from sitting on the Security Council? Only one, the Jewish nation. Then, in 2003, when the European Union polled people across the continent and asked which country represented the greatest threat to world peace, guess how almost 60% responded. Iran? North Korea? Russia? Pakistan? Syria? No. The answer was Israel! Israel, a thriving democracy of five and a half million Jews in the Middle Eastern sea of twenty totalitarian regimes with over 250 million Muslims, is the greatest threat to world peace. Go figure.

In this prayer, when we ask God to "grant honor to Your nation," we are praying for a global transformation. In truth, such a transformation would not be at all unreasonable. Consider the following.

> The Jews started it all—and by 'it' I mean so many of the things we care about, the underlying values that make all of us, Jew and Gentile, believer and atheist, tick. Without the Jews, we would see the world through different eyes, hear with different ears, even feel with different feelings . . . we would think with a different mind. And we would set a different course for our lives.
>
> —Thomas Cahill, *The Gifts of the Jews*

> It is almost beyond our capacity to imagine how the world would have fared if they [the Jews] had never

emerged. Certainly, the world without the Jews would have been a radically different place. Humanity might have eventually stumbled upon all the Jewish insights. But we cannot be sure. To them we owe the idea of equality before the law, sanctity of life, dignity of the human person, social responsibility, peace as an ideal, and many other items which constitute the basic furniture of the human mind. Without Jews it might have been a much emptier place.

—Paul Johnson, author,
A History of the Jews and A History of Christianity

They [the Jews] were the first people to arrive at an abstract notion of God. No people has produced a greater historical impact from such comparatively insignificant origins and resources. . .

—J.M. Roberts, *History of the World*

In the previous paragraph of the Amidah, we expressed our deepest desire for a world that would finally recognize God as the benevolent Creator of the universe. Now, on the heels of that hoped for recognition of reality, we pray that the world recognize that the Jewish people has a special role to play in God's creation, and that the Jewish role and the Jewish mission, is good for all Mankind.

INSIGHTS

לְעַמֶּךָ - *Your* nation. In our prayer for collective honor, we are not seeking any medals or to be enshrined in any Hall of Fame; rather, we are praying for reality-based sanity. Imagine an adolescent who is absolutely convinced that he is much wiser than his parents and who, for decades, scoffs at his parents' arcane way of thinking and doing things. Then, one day, it finally dawns on him that his greatest potential asset in life was the very people he scorned and rejected.

As Jews, we see ourselves as having the esteemed privilege of representing God in this world. It's true, we've done it with both hands tied behind our backs, but that's not what drives our prayer for respect. What drives us is that all we ever wanted was for God to get a little respect in this world. As Jews, we recognize that everything good we have achieved, every priceless contribution we have made to civilization, was only possible because of our relationship with God.

REFLECTION

Over twenty-four hundred years ago, the prophet Isaiah taught, "Nation shall not lift up sword against nation, and neither shall they study war any more." Those words, spoken in the midst of a world that glorified gladiators, the sword, and the warrior, were remarkably revolutionary. Today, if you are a person who is concerned about AIDS in Africa, oppression in Tibet, and victims of Hurricane Katrina, it's because the Torah taught us all to "pursue justice" and "love your neighbor as yourself."

If these values are defining parts of who you are, then reflect for a moment on where they came from. Like life itself, our most precious values and ideals are something to be grateful for. After all, world peace was God's idea you know, not Alfred Nobel's.

תְּהִלָּה לִירֵאֶיךָ - Praise to those who fear You. The Hebrew word for "fear," *yira*, also means "to see."

The question is this: What am I *seeing* when I make decisions in life? What core factors and values act as the guideposts that shape my decisions and behaviors? Is it a search for the greatest financial gain or for personal recognition that drives me? Is it power or physical gratification that I am *seeing* at the end of the road? Or, is what I *see*, and what I am looking at, God? Am I always *looking* to answer the question, "What does God want of me today?"

There is nothing wrong with being a great actor, business person, or athlete; but as Jews we pray to live in a world that praises people who are driven, first and foremost, by their desire to do good: to do what is right, holy, honest, straight, and beautiful in the eyes of God.

וְתִקְוָה טוֹבָה לְדוֹרְשֶׁיךָ - Good hope to those who are searching for You. "Those who are searching" are people who are yearning and striving to connect with God in a deep way. Imagine a young child who survived the Holocaust and then comes to America as an orphan: no family, no language, nothing. The cards are stacked against him. Everything about his circumstances says, "This kid doesn't have a chance." The truth is, America at its best, sees itself as a land of opportunity for everyone, regardless of background and circumstance.

Well, today we are praying for a world where the deck is stacked in favor of those searching for God. We pray that people in search of meaning and spirituality have reason to be hopeful and optimistic.

We want the same thing for our own personal inner world. We want our inner world to be conducive to searching for God, and that begins with being a searcher. So ask God: "Please help me stay focused on what I want in life: spirituality, use of my potential, a commitment to truth, devotion to friends, and closeness to those I love. Please God, make the circumstances of my world favorable to my search for meaning, goodness, and integrity—for You."

וּפִתְחוֹן פֶּה לַמְיַחֲלִים לָךְ - An open mouth for those who yearn for You. There are times when I can tell by the look on my son's face that he wants to ask me something, but he's hesitating. Inside he is so convinced that his request will be met with a resounding "no" that he can't even bring himself to open his mouth and ask.

Sometimes, perhaps often, we feel the same way. There is so much we want, but we feel that the possibilities are so terribly remote that it's a waste of time to make an effort, let alone ask for assistance. God, however, is the ultimate loving parent, so we need to ask. It's Rosh Hashanah—a new year, a new creation, a new beginning—and anything is possible. The road to our new reality begins with asking. So go ahead, ask God for what you truly want: ask Him for what's buried deep within your heart. Ask.

לַמְיַחֲלִים לָךְ - Those who yearn for You. Remember how the first human being was created in a barren world? (see page 12) Well, one of the reasons we were created in such an empty place, is to teach us that there is nothing in the world we can't ask for. We are each a world unto ourselves, and often we look at Your world and wonder, "How can I ever be close to God? how can God possibly ever love someone like me? how can I ever achieve what God wants me to achieve?" The answer begins with asking—so ask with all your heart. "God, I want to be close. I want to sense Your presence in my life. I want to live a life that I and You, can be proud of. God, I'm desperately longing to live my life on a higher spiritual plane. Please help me."

שִׂמְחָה לְאַרְצֶךָ, וְשָׂשׂוֹן לְעִירֶךָ - Joy to Your land and rejoicing to Your city. Two thousand years ago, the holy Temple in Jerusalem was destroyed, tens of thousands of Jews were slaughtered, and the Jewish people was driven into a long, dark exile. For two thousand years, Jews have watched as our holiest places were desecrated and churches and mosques were built on the ruins of the Temple. For two thousand years, we hoped and prayed for what seemed to be impossible—our return to Israel. Then, on May 14, 1948, a Jewish state was reestablished in Israel, and Jews around the world danced in the streets. Suddenly, that long-awaited return seemed to be unfolding before our very eyes. That very same day, seven Arab armies invaded Israel with the goal of crushing the newly reborn country, but they failed. When the guns finally fell silent, Israel had survived, though most of Jerusalem, including the Temple Mount and the Western Wall (the Kotel) were captured by Jordan. For the next nineteen years, the Jordanians allowed no Jews to pray at the Western Wall, desecrated Jewish cemeteries in Jerusalem, and destroyed every synagogue in the area under their control. Then, in June 1967, with united Arab armies again poised to wipe out the Jewish state, Israel won an astonishing war in just six days. In the course of that war, Israel captured the Temple Mount and the Western Wall. Once again, Jews everywhere cried, and danced, and were overwhelmed with a sense of joy and thanksgiving. Listen to the voices that still echo from that time:

> Slowly, slowly I began to approach the Wall. I approached it as a messenger of my grandfather and great grandfather and of all the generations in all the exiles who had never merited seeing it—and so they had sent me to represent them. I put my hand on the stones and the tears that started to flow were not my tears. They were the tears of all Israel.
>
> —Moshe Amirav, a paratrooper

> There was the Wall. I had never seen it before, but it was an old friend. I closed my eyes and brought my lips to the Wall. Tears burst forth. A Jewish soldier in the State of Israel is kissing history with his lips. Past, present and future all in one kiss. A soldier near me mumbled in disbelief, "We are at the Wall, at the Wall."
>
> —Abraham Duvdevani, a soldier

Today, two millennia of dreams and hopes and prayers are still unfolding. The Jewish people, the land of Israel, and our precious Jerusalem are still a work in progress. Our journey is still winding its way to completion, and tragically, the joy of the Jewish people in our homeland, is often mixed with bitterness, war, and terror.

So we pray: we pray that in the land of Israel, and the city of Jerusalem, there be *only* joy—overwhelming joy. More than ever, we know that this complete joy is possible, because more than once we have seen the impossible come to pass.

It's time now to join an endless torrent of prayers that has been flowing from Jewish hearts for thousands of years. It's time to pray that innocent Jewish children will be able to walk the streets of Israel with no fear that a missile may be launched their way at any moment. It's time to pray that Jewish mothers don't need to fear that a hate-indoctrinated Arab child might blow himself up in the local mall while her children are shopping for shoes. It's time to pray that the rebuilding of our Temple soon become a reality built on a backdrop of peace and tranquility. It's time to pray that Jewish hearts and souls everywhere unite as one, in Jerusalem.

"Joy to Your land and rejoicing to Your city," is a prayer that compresses all of Jewish history into one moment, one breath, and one heartbeat—one timeless, aching, inner longing—a longing for joy.

וּצְמִיחַת קֶרֶן - A sprouting shoot. Judaism believes in a Messianic era: a time when awareness of God will flow from Jerusalem and inspire the world like never before. We now allow our yearnings to soar even higher as we begin to envision the approach of that ultimate future.

A sprout, the earliest stage of visible life, represents slow, steady, yet almost unperceivable growth. At this moment in the Amidah, we find ourselves in the midst of a prayer for a grand, qualitative shift in the spiritual condition of the Jewish people. We have prayed for spiritual consciousness to permeate mankind, and for a world that is conducive to spiritual ambitions. We then prayed for true joy in our land: a joy that flows from the flourishing relationship of the Jewish people to God. We now pray for the future to begin to push its way through the soil of history, and to witness the blossoming dream of the Jewish people—the Messianic era.

לְדָוִד עַבְדֶּךָ - King David Your servant. Lake Placid is a small village of a few thousand souls nestled in the Adirondack Mountains of upstate New York. On March 21, 1928, Dr. Godfrey Dewey, a winter sports enthusiast, stood up at a joint meeting of the Lake Placid Kiwanis Club, Chamber of Commerce, and Municipal Board to propose that the village host the 1932 winter Olympics. People were incredulous, but Dr. Dewey was determined. After convincing the town elders that "Anything St. Moritz can do we can do better," Dr. Dewey sailed to Switzerland to make his pitch to the International Olympic Committee. Though Lake Placid was nowhere near ready for the task ahead, the good Doctor convinced the committee that Lake Placid, and not Montreal, Oslo or Lake Tahoe, would be the ideal venue for the Olympic games. When Dr. Dewey returned with the nomination in hand, the townspeople galvanized around his vision, and three years later, 364 athletes from seventeen countries participated in the opening ceremonies at the Olympic Stadium in Lake Placid. Isn't it incredible what selfless, inspired leadership can achieve?

When we refer to King David as "Your servant," what we are focusing on is the possibility of Jewish leadership that is completely and selflessly dedicated to God's agenda for the Jewish people. Imagine Jewish leadership that wanted nothing more than to see every Jew access his or her unique spiritual potential, and whose overarching priority was to inspire the Jewish nation to fulfill its purpose as a "Light unto the nations." When it comes to Jewish leadership and potential, we say to ourselves and to God—"Anything the townspeople of Lake Placid can do, we can do better."

REFLECTION

"Preparation of the lamp."

One kind of light can illuminate a dark room, but there is another kind of light, the kind that can illuminate a darkened heart. There is no shortage of darkness in the world; of families without hope, of broken lives, of people who are languishing in loneliness. Each of us has the ability to be a lamp, a source of light. There is no better day than today, and no better moment than now, to look inside and ask, "Where do I see darkness? what can I do to alleviate it? how can I prepare myself to be a source of light?" Each of us can be a light to the whole world when we bring some light into the darkened world of just one person.

וּבְכֵן, צַדִּיקִים יִרְאוּ וְיִשְׂמָחוּ, וִישָׁרִים יַעֲלֹזוּ, וַחֲסִידִים בְּרִנָּה
יָגִילוּ. וְעוֹלָתָה תִּקְפָּץ פִּיהָ, וְכָל הָרִשְׁעָה כֻּלָּהּ כֶּעָשָׁן תִּכְלֶה,
כִּי תַעֲבִיר מֶמְשֶׁלֶת זָדוֹן מִן הָאָרֶץ.

➔ *Amidah continues on page 102*

AND ALSO, THEN, THE RIGHTEOUS . . .

And also, then, the righteous will see (this world) and rejoice, the straight will exult, and the devout will express their jubilance with song.

Injustice will shut its mouth and all wickedness will vanish like smoke, when You remove tyrannical regimes from the earth.

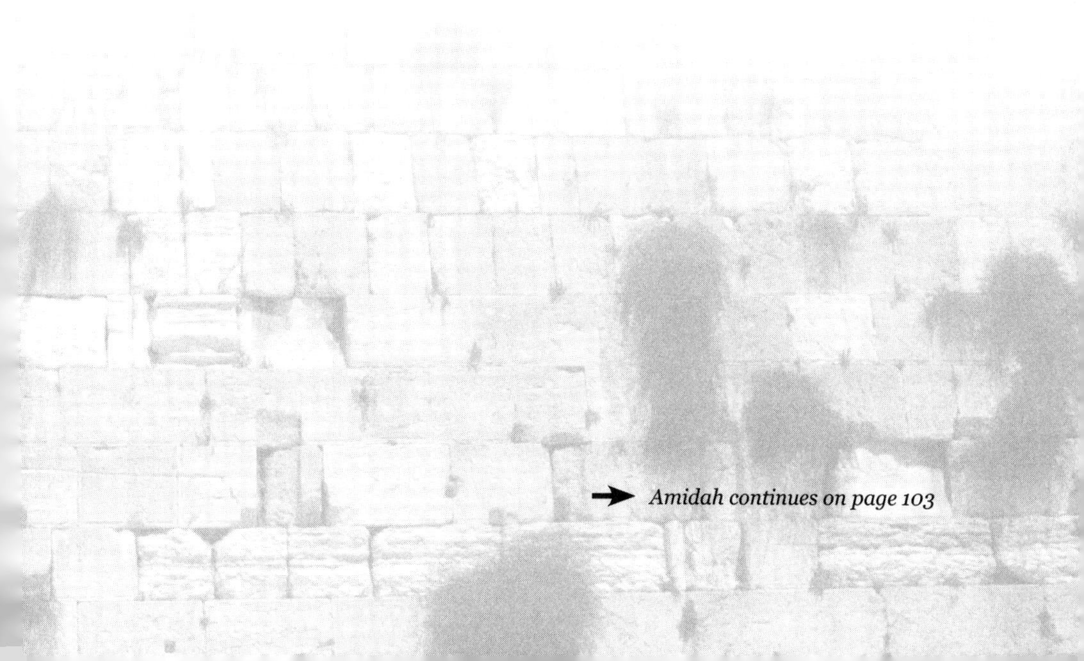

➔ *Amidah continues on page 103*

THE BIG PICTURE

Visualize success. Successful entrepreneurs do it, Tiger Woods does it, and it's what this paragraph is about. This portion of the Amidah is more of a projection, or visualization, than a request. What we are about to do is look at the world through the transformed lens that is the outgrowth of the last two paragraphs of prayer. First we prayed for a world that was elevated by a universal God focused consciousness. Then, we prayed for a world in which the Jewish people fulfilled their role as a light unto the nations. Now what we do is place ourselves in that transformed world, and imagine what it would look like.

Consider this: We have all been witness to horrors. The horror of 9/11, of a government that starves its own citizens, of rockets being launched randomly every day at Jewish cities in Israel, and of relentless slaughter in Darfur. There is no shortage of brutal, inhumane horror in the world. But what if one day it all stopped. No more terror and murder, no more malicious starvation, no more indoctrinating children to hate and murder other children—no more. What if the seemingly intractable human impulse to horror vanished like a puff of smoke? What if "All wickedness will vanish like a puff of smoke?"

At this moment in our prayers, as we stand at the threshold of a new year, we envision the potential for a completely different world, a world free of horror. And, as we visualize this world and open our hearts to its magnificent potential, we begin to feel a deep longing for that reality. We begin to feel that *this* is the kind of world we truly want to live in.

There is a deeply resonant power in this paragraph, the power of a timeless melody: an eternal melody. It is as if this paragraph dares us to dream again, only this time bigger than ever.

So let's do just that: let's allow the vision nestled in these words to carry us aloft to a place where we look out on a world free of evil, treachery, and self-centeredness. Let's envision a world where holy people will walk the streets and rejoice because everywhere they look they see only beauty—only kindness, caring, and love—only sweet goodness.

When we dream, we yearn, and at this moment our yearnings become our prayers.

INSIGHTS

צַדִּיקִים יִרְאוּ וְיִשְׂמָחוּ, וִישָׁרִים יַעֲלֹזוּ, וַחֲסִידִים בְּרִנָּה יָגִילוּ - **The righteous will rejoice, the straight will exult, and the devout will express their jubilance with song.** One way to nudge the world closer to becoming the world of our dreams, is to get up off our chairs and get-out-there-and-do-something. There is an additional way to help the world progress: by improving ourselves and by drawing out more and more of our own latent potential for beauty and goodness. There is a kabbalistic concept (see page 33 for a more lengthy discussion of this idea) that teaches how each of us is like a tuning fork. With our actions, we emit spiritual waves, like the musical notes that sound when one strikes a tuning fork.

God designed creation in such a way that man's free-willed actions have a direct impact on the transcendental forces that are the inner workings of the universe. This is true not only of actions but even words and thoughts . . . " (Rabbi Moshe Chaim Luzzato, 18th century kabbalist, *The Way of God* 1:5)

Sometimes we can see how our choices, words, and actions have a positive influence on other people, but often times we can't. At a very deep level of reality, the spiritual waves that flow from us have an impact on the world that is beyond the realm of perception. Our efforts to grow and refine who we are, in some way, also refine the world.

This paragraph speaks of three kinds of people: the righteous, the straight, and the devout. These three people are three stages of personal growth. For us, they are guiding lights that represent the stages of moral and spiritual growth that we can each strive for.

צַדִּיקִים - **Righteous.** A righteous person is someone who knows that life is a constant struggle to grow, and who doesn't shy away from the challenge. Every day he or she looks at life and says: "I know that today is another day of tension between the higher calling of my soul and my body's willingness to settle for mediocrity, and I'm not going to capitulate to my desire for comfort. I'm going to strive to grow, to challenge myself, and to reach for greatness." A righteous person accepts life's challenges and tries to choose the spiritual over the mundane, the kind over the selfish, and the right over the wrong.

וִישָׁרִים - **Straight.** People who rise to the very highest levels of accomplishment are people who have transcended the urge to take-the-easy-way-out. The thought of settling for mediocrity is no longer part of their lexicon; they are singularly focused on, "How can I continue to improve, how can I extract more of my potential out of life, and how can today be better than yesterday?" For the straight person, the issue is not will I or won't I grow; rather, the attitude is, "Just show me the best way to wring more of my potential out of life and I'm ready, because that is all I'm interested in."

וַחֲסִידִים - **Devout.** The devout person begins where the straight one finishes. She is not only committed to doing what's right, or whatever is required for her to grow, she also wants to go the extra mile. If a sick neighbor needs help with dinner, she doesn't just want to cook a nice meal, she wants to organize all the neighbors to pitch in for a week. In her personal life, in her interactions with other people, and in her relationship with God, she doesn't just want to grow and climb higher, she wants to soar far beyond what most people would ever demand of themselves.

REFLECTION

To be Jewish is to be committed to a path of personal growth, and growth is always challenging. Each of our lives is complex and multi-dimensional. In some areas of life we are doing great; other areas are a huge battle, and in some areas we haven't even begun the struggle.

Now is a good time to look at areas of your life and evaluate which category they fall under. The following brief exercise will help you introspect, evaluate, and grow. What you are going to do is identify aspects of your life, give them a grade, and then consider ways you can realistically nudge yourself, and the world, towards a higher place in the coming year.

We will use the following grading system:

A = devout.

B = straight.

C = righteous.

D = I really need to start doing something about this.

E = Right now, this is beyond me, maybe I'll address it next year.

Some areas of life to reflect on:

- *My relationship with my spouse, parents, siblings, children, other family members, and close friends.*
- *Relationships with other people like my boss, co-workers, employees, and other people I interact with on a regular basis.*
- *My sensitivity to the needs of my fellow Jews in Israel who have been victimized by terror or who live under the threat of a missile attack.*
- *My efforts to learn more about Judaism and grow as a Jew.*
- *My effort to be aware of God as I go through my daily activities.*
- *My honesty and integrity in business.*
- *My sensitivity to the needs of poor people in my community.*
- *Character traits like: patience, anger, listening to others, honesty, self-control, humility, gratefulness, hate, generosity, perseverance, and joyfulness.*

וְתִמְלוֹךְ, אַתָּה יהוה לְבַדֶּךָ, עַל כָּל מַעֲשֶׂיךָ, בְּהַר צִיּוֹן מִשְׁכַּן
: כְּבוֹדֶךָ, וּבִירוּשָׁלַיִם עִיר קָדְשֶׁךָ, כַּכָּתוּב בְּדִבְרֵי קָדְשֶׁךָ:
יִמְלֹךְ יהוה לְעוֹלָם, אֱלֹהַיִךְ צִיּוֹן לְדֹר וָדֹר, הַלְלוּיָהּ.

→ *Amidah continues on page 108*

↠ And then You alone will reign . . .

And then You alone, Adonai, will reign over all Your works, on Mount Zion, dwelling place of Your Presence; and in Jerusalem, Your holy city, as it is written in Your holy words: "Adonai will reign forever—Zion, Your God—from generation to generation. Praise God."

➔ *Amidah continues on page 109*

THE BIG PICTURE

The answer to the question, "If a tree falls in the woods and there is no one around to hear the sound, did it make a noise?" is yes. Likewise, the answer to the question, "If there is a King of the universe but no one notices Him, is He really there?" is yes. However, the difference between a world in which no one notices the King, and a world where everyone notices Him, is the difference between night and day. In one world darkness reigns, and in the other there is light—the light of God's presence.

Let's try a little exercise.

Close your eyes and imagine that you are standing all alone at the top of a mountain. A slight breeze is blowing, huge clouds hang in the sky, and for as far as you can see there is nothing but rocky mountain peaks jutting into an endless blue sky.

Now open your eyes.

It's time to turn off your imagination, and return to wherever you are, which probably isn't on top of a mountain.

Was that mountain real, or was it just the stuff of your imagination? The answer is both. On the one hand there *was* some reality to that mountain, so much so that it could actually produce the feeling of being there. At the same time, it *was* just your imagination, and whatever reality it had was completely dependent on you. As long as you were choosing to focus your mind on those clouds, they would hang in the sky. However, the moment you focused elsewhere, the clouds would simply cease to exist. In a sense, this is a description of God's relationship to all of existence: God—the King of the universe—*wills*, and we exist.

The Jewish understanding of reality is that creation was not a one-time event. Rather, God is creating everything anew at each and every moment. Beneath the surface of *all* existence there is only One true existence, the Creator. The ongoing Will of the King sustains everything that exists—everything—

at every moment. If you reflect on this idea and let it fill your consciousness, you can begin to sense the presence of God in every moment and every thing: in every person around you, and in every breath you take. If all people would reflect on this idea, and take it to heart, then the world we live in would be a radically different place. It would become the palace of the King, a palace filled with light.

INSIGHTS

עַל כָּל מַעֲשֶׂיךָ - God, will reign over all Your works. Here again we go beyond the personal and focus our prayers on a universal theme. For God's reign to be complete, so to speak, His reality must be recognized and accepted by all of humanity, and that is exactly what we are praying for.

עַל כָּל מַעֲשֶׂיךָ - over all Your works. Each of us was fashioned by God, and each of us has the potential for a relationship with God. Each of us is a vital, unique, and beautiful part of "all" God has made. We want the whole world to be filled with God's presence, and we want each of our worlds to be filled with God's presence. In truth, that presence is with us at every moment: all we need to do is open our eyes and hearts and we will become aware of the reality that surrounds us—we will realize that we are living in the palace of the King.

בְּהַר צִיּוֹן . . . וּבִירוּשָׁלַיִם - Mount Zion . . . Jerusalem. Abraham entered into an eternal covenant with God that forever committed his descendants, the Jewish nation, to be God's representatives in this world. The Land of Israel is where that covenant is to be lived and fulfilled. The city of Jerusalem is the heart of Israel, and Zion is like Jerusalem's soul.

After the Exodus from Egypt, the Jewish people were told, "And you shall make for Me a *Mishkan* (holy Sanctuary) and My Presence will be manifest among you." (Exodus 25:8) This

Mishkan-Sanctuary was built in the desert and traveled with the Jewish people until it finally reached its permanent residence in Jerusalem.

Jerusalem and Zion are two aspects of the Jewish people's relationship with God. Just like every husband and wife has an inner private life, and an outer, more public life, the same is true with the Jewish nation. Mount Zion and the Temple (*Beit HaMikdosh*) are the inner sanctum of the deepest spiritual intimacy between God and the Jewish people. Jerusalem, on the other hand, is a city, and cities are public places. Jerusalem is a city—a holy city—where the Jewish people's relationship to God is expressed in the course of everyday life. Jerusalem is the place where the deep relationship between God and the Jewish people expresses itself to the outside world.

REFLECTION

For thousands of years, Jews prayed to go to Jerusalem, though very few realized their dream. If you are one of the fortunate ones who have been to Jerusalem, then you know that there is something of incomparable and indescribable beauty there—your soul surely knows it. You now have an opportunity to reconnect. To do that, I suggest you go to the Kotel. Are you ready? Good, let's go.

Close your eyes, take a few deep, calming breaths, and when you are ready, see yourself walking towards the Kotel. You may want to start your walk from the top of the steps in the Jewish Quarter; maybe from the bus stop, or perhaps in the Kotel plaza. If it is daytime, be sure to take notice of the clear blue sky. If it is late at night, feel the crisp air and listen for those lone echoes of prayer rising to the star-filled heavens. Now, walk slowly to the Wall and stop just inches away. Feel its presence all around you and within you. Slowly lift your hand to touch those precious stones. Kiss them. You are there. Allow the Kotel and Jerusalem and Zion to open your heart. From there, you can speak to God—you can pour your heart out. Go ahead: whatever comes to mind, whatever stirs within you, whatever whispers—from Yerushalayim.

If you want to face yourself, face the Wall.
If you want to see your life more clearly, come here and close your eyes.
—Sarah Shapiro, author

WE CAN STILL GIVE . . .

"It's easy to forget that we have an incredible ability to love one another."

Due to a catastrophic misdiagnosis, Ruthee has been paralyzed from the waist down since 2005.

"I had a choice, to pull in or to reach out. I can still be kind to people. I can still reach out. I can still ease other people's burdens. God said, 'Love your neighbor.' Don't ever stop reaching out."

CHOOSE LIFE

קָדוֹשׁ אַתָּה וְנוֹרָא שְׁמֶךָ, וְאֵין אֱלוֹהַּ מִבַּלְעָדֶיךָ, כַּכָּתוּב:
וַיִּגְבַּהּ יהוה צְבָאוֹת בַּמִּשְׁפָּט, וְהָאֵל הַקָּדוֹשׁ נִקְדַּשׁ
בִּצְדָקָה. בָּרוּךְ אַתָּה יהוה, הַמֶּלֶךְ הַקָּדוֹשׁ.

→ *Amidah continues on page 114*

✤ Holy is what You are . . .

Holy is what You are; and Your Name is awesome, and there is no god other than You, as it is written: "Adonai, Master of all heavenly creations, through Your judgment of the world You will be exalted, and the Almighty Holy One, through righteousness You will be sanctified."

Blessed are You, Adonai, the King who is the Holy One.

➔ *Amidah continues on page 115*

THE BIG PICTURE

The Hebrew word for "holy" is *kadosh. Kadosh* means "separate" or 'distinct." In Jewish thought, the word *kadosh* implies something that distinguishes itself by virtue of the fact that it is connected to a higher realm of spirituality. A Jewish marriage is called *kadosh* because a marriage is more than just a partnership: it's the shared commitment a couple makes to attach their life—their goals, values, and aspirations—to something higher. The land of Israel is called *kadosh*, holy, because it is distinct from all other lands in that it possesses a unique, inherent quality that enables people to connect to God.

When we say that God is *kadosh*, we mean that the nature of His Being is something totally different and distinct from anything else that exists. In fact, God is unfathomable. This is why.

We live in a 3-D world of stunning variety and beauty, but God doesn't. In our world there is length, height, and width; the three dimensions that make space, and therefore physical matter, possible. Remove any one of those dimensions and space itself disappears. Go ahead, try it: try imagining a room with just length and width. Now think about how much furniture you could squeeze into that heightless room. You will realize that even a chair the size of a molecule won't fit, because a room with no height is a room with no space: none, zero. Now try this. Imagine if your spaceless room existed in a dimension where there was no time—no past, no future, and even no present. Hard to imagine, isn't it? Well, God exists outside of space, outside of anything physical, outside of time, and outside of everything else we can conceive of. That is just the beginning of what it means that God is *kadosh*: He is separate and distinct in a way that is entirely beyond comprehension.

There is, however, something else we need to know that is equally mind-boggling. Somehow, some way, it's possible for us 3-D folks to have a relationship with God. After all, that is what today is all about. On Rosh Hashanah it's as if God is saying to us, "Look, I know this seems impossible, but trust Me. When I created you, and when I gave you a soul, I gave you the ability to bridge our two worlds. You can do it, and I am here waiting—right next to you."

INSIGHTS

קָדוֹשׁ אַתָּה וְנוֹרָא שְׁמֶךָ - You are holy and Your Name is awesome. In Hebrew, the word for "name," and the word for "there" have the same root. "There" implies that you can point to something and clearly identify where and what it is. That is also the function of a name. A name enables you to identify exactly who you are speaking about. In Jewish thought, God has many names, but in truth, none of them even begin to capture the slightest bit of His essence.

When we say that God is holy (*kadosh*), and that His Name is awesome, what we mean is this: while God is utterly different and distinct from us, there are times when He does have a "name," so to speak. There are times when we can discern some of God's involvement and presence in the world, and in our lives. At those moments, even an inkling of God's presence is awesome. The little bits that we can perceive, are tiny windows that afford us a glimpse of the breathtaking reality that lies beyond the horizon of our limited view.

וַיִּגְבַּה . . . בַּמִּשְׁפָּט - Lofty in judgment. On Rosh Hashanah, God scrutinizes the world and "sits in judgment." Judaism is unequivocal when it comes to right and wrong. God, the Creator of all existence, knows what is good and bad for the world He created. When God taught us that stealing and incest are bad, and giving a portion of one's income to the poor is good, He wasn't just stating an opinion—He was defining moral reality. In searching for morality, people are actually searching for God.

To acknowledge that God is the source of right and wrong is to recognize that morality derives from the "loftiest" source possible. When God judges us, He's not being a tyrant, rather it is as if He were saying, "I created you and I know your great potential. I know even better than you know how good you can be, and what heights you can reach. When I sit in judgment it is only because I care about you, believe in you, and am concerned about the entire world—and you."

REFLECTION

Parents care about their children's hygiene, grades, and sense of honesty because they love them. For a parent to ignore a child's behavior is to deliver the most devastating of all messages: "You don't matter." Rosh Hashanah, the Day of Judgment, is when we know that God loves us. He cares about how we have lived, and how we will live. If you have ever struggled with low self-esteem, Rosh Hashanah is the perfect antidote for wounded self-worth. Take a moment and allow the awareness of God's love to sink in. It's okay: let it wash over you. God wants you—yes, little you—to feel His caring Presence.

EAT DESSERT FIRST . . .

As often as she can, Irene visits lonely patients at South Nassau Community Hospital. Using her wheelchair to go from room to room, she visits twenty to thirty people a day.

"Rosh Hashanah has always been a time of gratefulness to God for all that I have. It is an opportunity to pray to God to help His troubled planet, to help us in choosing the spiritual in all aspects of life, and in using the Torah as our guide book."

Diabolical experiments were carried out on over three thousand sets of twins in Auschwitz. Less than two hundred of those children survived. Irene and her brother are two of them. The bumper sticker on the back of her wheelchair reads, "Life is short. Eat dessert first."

CHOOSE LIFE

✤ קְדוּשַּׁת הַיּוֹם - SANCTITY OF THE DAY ✤

אַתָּה בְחַרְתָּנוּ מִכָּל הָעַמִּים, אָהַבְתָּ אוֹתָנוּ, וְרָצִיתָ בָּנוּ, וְרוֹמַמְתָּנוּ מִכָּל הַלְּשׁוֹנוֹת, וְקִדַּשְׁתָּנוּ בְּמִצְוֹתֶיךָ. וְקֵרַבְתָּנוּ מַלְכֵּנוּ לַעֲבוֹדָתֶךָ, וְשִׁמְךָ הַגָּדוֹל וְהַקָּדוֹשׁ עָלֵינוּ קָרָאתָ.

(On Saturday night only, add the following paragraph. On all other nights, continue to the next paragraph.)

וַתּוֹדִיעֵנוּ יהוה אֱלֹהֵינוּ אֶת מִשְׁפְּטֵי צִדְקֶךָ, וַתְּלַמְּדֵנוּ לַעֲשׂוֹת (בָּהֶם) חֻקֵּי רְצוֹנֶךָ. וַתִּתֶּן לָנוּ יהוה אֱלֹהֵינוּ מִשְׁפָּטִים יְשָׁרִים וְתוֹרוֹת אֱמֶת חֻקִּים וּמִצְוֹת טוֹבִים. וַתַּנְחִילֵנוּ זְמַנֵּי שָׂשׂוֹן וּמוֹעֲדֵי קֹדֶשׁ וְחַגֵּי נְדָבָה. וַתּוֹרִישֵׁנוּ קְדֻשַּׁת שַׁבָּת וּכְבוֹד מוֹעֵד וַחֲגִיגַת הָרֶגֶל. וַתַּבְדֵּל יהוה אֱלֹהֵינוּ בֵּין קֹדֶשׁ לְחוֹל, בֵּין אוֹר לְחֹשֶׁךְ, בֵּין יִשְׂרָאֵל לָעַמִּים, בֵּין יוֹם הַשְּׁבִיעִי לְשֵׁשֶׁת יְמֵי הַמַּעֲשֶׂה. בֵּין קְדֻשַּׁת שַׁבָּת לִקְדֻשַּׁת יוֹם טוֹב הִבְדַּלְתָּ, וְאֶת יוֹם הַשְּׁבִיעִי מִשֵּׁשֶׁת יְמֵי הַמַּעֲשֶׂה קִדַּשְׁתָּ, הִבְדַּלְתָּ וְקִדַּשְׁתָּ אֶת עַמְּךָ יִשְׂרָאֵל בִּקְדֻשָּׁתֶךָ.

(On Shabbat, add the words in brackets.)

וַתִּתֶּן לָנוּ יהוה אֱלֹהֵינוּ בְּאַהֲבָה אֶת יוֹם [הַשַּׁבָּת הַזֶּה וְאֶת יוֹם] הַזִּכָּרוֹן הַזֶּה, יוֹם [זִכְרוֹן] תְּרוּעָה [בְּאַהֲבָה] מִקְרָא קֹדֶשׁ, זֵכֶר לִיצִיאַת מִצְרָיִם.

➔ *Amidah continues on page 118*

✦ KEDUSHAT HAYOM - SANCTITY OF THE DAY ✦

You have chosen us from among all the nations. You loved us and took pleasure in us.

You elevated us above all the other languages and you made us holy through your commandments. You drew us close, Our King, to Your service, and You have associated Your great and holy name with us.

(On Saturday night only, add the following two paragraphs. On all other nights, continue to the next paragraph.)

You made known to us, Adonai, our God, Your righteous laws, and You have taught us to do the edicts of Your will. And You gave us, Adonai our God, just and equitable laws and teachings of truth, good edicts and commandments. You gave us as a heritage, seasons of rejoicing, appointed holidays of holiness and the voluntary offerings of the festivals. And You bequeathed to us the holiness of Shabbat, the weighty significance of the appointed holiday and the celebration of the festival.

And You distinguished, Adonai our God, between the holy and the mundane, between light and darkness, between Israel and the other nations, between the seventh day and the six days of work. Between the (special) holiness of Shabbat and the holiness of the holiday You have distinguished. And the seventh day, from amidst the six work days, You have made holy. You designated and invested with holiness—Your nation Israel—with Your holiness.

(On Shabbat, add the words in brackets.)

And You gave us, Adonai our God, out of love, [this Shabbat day and] this Day of Remembering, a day for [the remembrance of] sounding the shofar [out of love] a day designated by holiness—commemorating the Exodus from Egypt.

➔ *Amidah continues on page 119*

THE BIG PICTURE

It's true, we are the Chosen people.

Over three thousand years ago, though people believed in crocodiles, sheep, and the sacred scarab, they were totally clueless when it came to knowing that there was one God, and that God is *One*. Then, one day, Abraham showed up and came to the unique realization that there is only one God, one Creator, and one possible source of meaning in life. As you can imagine, God was thrilled when someone finally noticed Him, so He chose Abraham to be His partner and emissary to Mankind. We, the descendents of Abraham, are the inheritors of that partnership.

The job of being the Chosen people isn't easy, but it does come with some great spiritual perks. While God loves and cares about all people, we are privileged to have a unique connection—a special relationship. This special relationship expresses itself in commandments (*mitzvot*), holidays, and observances that enable us to rise to the challenge of our chosenness.

As individuals, there is nothing more uplifting and empowering than to know that we are loved by God. As Jews, there is nothing more uplifting and empowering than to know that we were chosen by God.

INSIGHTS

וְשִׁמְךָ הַגָּדוֹל וְהַקָּדוֹשׁ עָלֵינוּ קָרָאתָ - And You have associated Your great and holy name with us.

We as athletes are proud to have the honor of representing our countries.

—Charmaine Crooks,
five-time Canadian
olympic sprinter

It is virtually impossible for the behavior of an Olympic athlete, or a foreign diplomat, *not* to reflect, one way or another, on his or her country. As Jews, we have the honor of being "associated" with God: we are His ambassadors. Jews throughout the ages, and in every circumstance, have always declared our association with God to be the highest and most distinguished privilege.

בְּאַהֲבָה אֶת יוֹם הַזִּכָּרוֹן -
. . . out of love, this day of remembering. A child that is forgotten, is devastated.

I know a very successful man who was raised by a full-time domestic worker. She was a good and kind woman, but she wasn't his mother. "My parents never paid much attention," he told me, "they never really wanted me, and I was just sort of forgotten." With all his wealth, with his Manhattan penthouse and eye-grabbing motorcycle, the man remains deflated—forgotten by those who should have loved him.

God remembers us: today, and always. To God, we are always precious and never forgotten. We are always worthy of His attention, His love.

אֱלֹהֵינוּ וֵאלֹהֵי אֲבוֹתֵינוּ, יַעֲלֶה, וְיָבֹא, וְיַגִּיעַ, וְיֵרָאֶה, וְיֵרָצֶה,
וְיִשָּׁמַע, וְיִפָּקֵד, וְיִזָּכֵר זִכְרוֹנֵנוּ וּפִקְדוֹנֵנוּ, וְזִכְרוֹן אֲבוֹתֵינוּ,
וְזִכְרוֹן מָשִׁיחַ בֶּן דָּוִד עַבְדֶּךָ, וְזִכְרוֹן יְרוּשָׁלַיִם עִיר קָדְשֶׁךָ,
וְזִכְרוֹן כָּל עַמְּךָ בֵּית יִשְׂרָאֵל לְפָנֶיךָ, לִפְלֵיטָה לְטוֹבָה לְחֵן
וּלְחֶסֶד וּלְרַחֲמִים, לְחַיִּים וּלְשָׁלוֹם בְּיוֹם הַזִּכָּרוֹן הַזֶּה. זָכְרֵנוּ
יהוה אֱלֹהֵינוּ בּוֹ לְטוֹבָה, וּפָקְדֵנוּ בוֹ לִבְרָכָה, וְהוֹשִׁיעֵנוּ בוֹ
לְחַיִּים. וּבִדְבַר יְשׁוּעָה וְרַחֲמִים, חוּס וְחָנֵּנוּ וְרַחֵם עָלֵינוּ
וְהוֹשִׁיעֵנוּ, כִּי אֵלֶיךָ עֵינֵינוּ, כִּי אֵל מֶלֶךְ חַנּוּן וְרַחוּם אָתָּה.

→ *Amidah continues on page 122*

May there ascend, come and arrive . . .

Our God and God of our forefathers, allow there to ascend, come and arrive; and appear, be accepted and heard, be counted and remembered—our remembrance and our being noticed and counted—and the remembrance of our forefathers, and the remembrance of the Messiah, the son of David, Your servant; and the remembrance of Jerusalem Your holy city and the remembrance of Your entire nation , the Family of Israel, before You—for deliverance, well-being, favor, kindness and mercy; for life and peace on this Day of Remembering.

Remember us, Adonai our God, today, for goodness, and pay close attention to us, today, for blessing, and rescue us, today, for life. In keeping with the promise of deliverance and mercy, spare us and be pleased with us, have compassion on us and rescue us; for our eyes are turned in hope to You, because You are God, the gracious and merciful King.

➔ *Amidah continues on page 123*

THE BIG PICTURE

As God's people, we have been part of virtually every major chapter in human history. We have witnessed, endured, and accomplished so very much. Yet we know that there is so much more to come, that our history is still unfolding, and that we are still progressing towards a brilliant future.

Until the day when it finally happens, we will never stop praying for the entire nation of Israel to return to the land of Israel, and the holy city of Jerusalem. Until the day when it finally happens, we will never stop praying for all Jews to recognize and embrace the beauty of being Jewish, and the opportunity to connect with their soul's deepest yearnings. Until the day when it finally happens, we will never stop praying for the Jewish people to be united as one—one people with one heart—living together in harmony and peace. Until the day when it finally happens, we will never stop lifting our eyes in anticipation of the day when the King whose palace was burned to the ground, will restore His kingdom.

INSIGHTS

כָּל עַמְּךָ בֵּית יִשְׂרָאֵל - Your entire nation, the family of Israel . . . God never gives up on the Jewish people, and neither do we. After all, we're family.

The Kabbalistic teachings tell us that while individual Jews may be flawed, on the metaphysical plane—in the realm of the soul—there exists a pristine entity known as *Knesset Yisroel.* Knesset Yisroel is the spiritual equivalent of the-whole-is-greater-than-the-sum-of-its parts. Knesset Yisroel is the timeless, transcendent totality of the Jewish people.

We can all find faults with ourselves and with our fellow Jews; that's easy. However, if we step back and take a broad, panoramic look at the Jewish people and Jewish history, what we will discover is a masterpiece. Truthfully, it's not that hard to look at your community, at Israel, and at world Jewry and also find a gorgeous family portrait.

Today we pray for our *whole* family, and we pray for the absolute best.

REFLECTION

Did you ever have an experience where you felt profoundly connected to the Jewish people? Did you ever feel like meeting another Jew was somehow like meeting a relative you had never met before? Those experiences are doorways to a very special place. Recall those moments—what you thought and what you felt—and follow them. Step through that door of Jewish connection, and it will take you to a beautiful place.

אֱלֹהֵינוּ וֵאלֹהֵי אֲבוֹתֵינוּ, מְלוֹךְ עַל כָּל הָעוֹלָם כֻּלּוֹ בִּכְבוֹדֶךָ, וְהִנָּשֵׂא עַל כָּל הָאָרֶץ בִּיקָרֶךָ, וְהוֹפַע בַּהֲדַר גְּאוֹן עֻזֶּךָ, עַל כָּל יוֹשְׁבֵי תֵבֵל אַרְצֶךָ. וְיֵדַע כָּל פָּעוּל כִּי אַתָּה פְעַלְתּוֹ, וְיָבִין כָּל יָצוּר כִּי אַתָּה יְצַרְתּוֹ, וְיֹאמַר כֹּל אֲשֶׁר נְשָׁמָה בְאַפּוֹ, יהוה אֱלֹהֵי יִשְׂרָאֵל מֶלֶךְ, וּמַלְכוּתוֹ בַּכֹּל מָשָׁלָה.

(On Shabbat, add the words in brackets)

[אֱלֹהֵינוּ וֵאלֹהֵי אֲבוֹתֵינוּ, רְצֵה בִמְנוּחָתֵנוּ] קַדְּשֵׁנוּ בְּמִצְוֹתֶיךָ, וְתֵן חֶלְקֵנוּ בְּתוֹרָתֶךָ, שַׂבְּעֵנוּ מִטּוּבֶךָ, וְשַׂמְּחֵנוּ בִּישׁוּעָתֶךָ. [וְהַנְחִילֵנוּ, יהוה אֱלֹהֵינוּ, בְּאַהֲבָה וּבְרָצוֹן שַׁבַּת קָדְשֶׁךָ, וְיָנוּחוּ בָהּ יִשְׂרָאֵל מְקַדְּשֵׁי שְׁמֶךָ.] וְטַהֵר לִבֵּנוּ לְעָבְדְּךָ בֶּאֱמֶת. כִּי אַתָּה אֱלֹהִים אֱמֶת, וּדְבָרְךָ אֱמֶת וְקַיָּם לָעַד. בָּרוּךְ אַתָּה יהוה, מֶלֶךְ עַל כָּל הָאָרֶץ, מְקַדֵּשׁ [הַשַּׁבָּת וְ] יִשְׂרָאֵל וְיוֹם הַזִּכָּרוֹן.

➔ *Amidah continues on page 128*

✦ Reign over the entire universe . . .

Our God and God of our forefathers, reign over the entire universe, in Your esteemed honor; and be elevated over the entire earth in Your grandeur, and let Your eminence shine in the brilliance of Your majestic power over all who live in the settled regions of Your earth. So that everything that was made will know that You made it, and everything that was molded will understand that You molded it, and everything that has the breath of life (the soul) in its nostrils will say: "Adonai, God of Israel is King, and His kingdom reigns over everything."

(On Shabbat, add the words in brackets)

[Our God and God of our forefathers, be pleased with our rest] Make us holy through Your commandments and give us our unique portion in Your Torah; satisfy us from Your goodness and make us joyous in Your deliverance. [And give us our heritage Adonai, our God, with love and favor, Your holy Shabbat, and may Israel—the nation that sanctifies Your Name—rest on it.] And purify our hearts to serve You with true integrity, for You God are truth and Your word is true and endures forever.

Blessed are You, Adonai, King over the entire earth, Who sanctifies [the Shabbat and] Israel and the Day of Remembering.

➔ *Amidah continues on page 129*

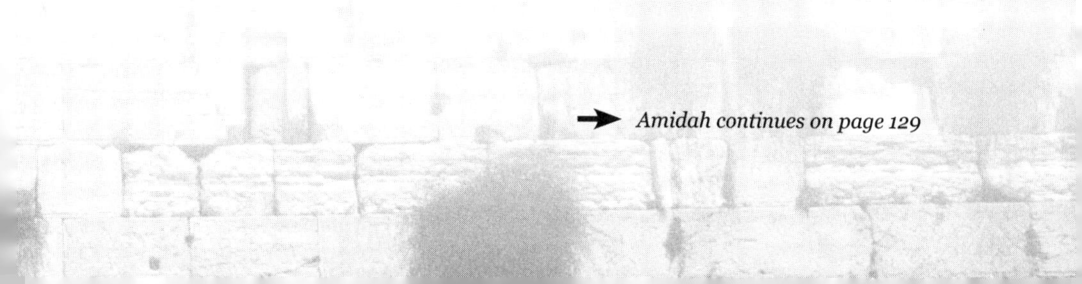

THE BIG PICTURE

The one word that captures the essence of Rosh Hashanah, is "King." In Hebrew, the word for king is *melech*. Though our prayers may seem to be about many things, in fact they are about one thing, our striving to recognize and embrace God's sovereignty. But what does that really mean? To embrace God as King means to understand, integrate, and commit to the foundational ideas and ideals that are at the core of the Jewish understanding of reality. So, in order to find our way to relating to the King, we need to understand the ideas that define the Jewish view of life.

Judaism begins with the seminal idea that God created everything that exists out of absolute nothingness, and that creation has a purpose. That purpose is for us to achieve the greatest meaning and pleasure possible. Anyone will tell you that if there is a God, a "King of the universe," then to have an experience of being in His presence would be life's ultimate peak experience. This realization is at the heart of the Jewish view of life—that the meaning of life comes from being connected to the Sovereign source of all existence—God Himself. The way we achieve our purpose is to develop a relationship with God, and, since God didn't want to leave us in the dark when it comes to developing that relationship, He gave us a manual. That manual is the Torah. The Torah is a guide for transforming every square inch of our potentially mundane lives into opportunities for greatness. The Torah is a detailed manual for how to infuse meaning, kindness, beauty, goodness, and spirituality into every moment of our lives. In the Jewish view, there isn't a dimension of life that isn't brimming with ultimate potential. There isn't a moment that we *can't* be in the King's presence.

When God gave the Torah to the Jewish people, He told us that it would transform us into a "Kingdom of spiritual role models (*Kohanim*) and a holy (*kadosh*) nation." In the kingdom of Israel, *all* the "subjects" in the realm are members of the royal family. The life of every Jew, and the collective life of the Jewish people, is meant to reflect the light of Godliness into the world. God is our King, we have the privilege of being His emissaries, and Jewish life is the path to fulfilling that grandest and most ennobling of all human endeavors.

To accept God as our King is to embrace this core paradigm for Jewish living. To pray for the recognition of God's sovereignty is to pray for a world that lives with its eyes, heart, and soul wide open to the reality of God's Presence.

INSIGHTS

כָּל יָצוּר - **Everything that was molded.** Everything that exists was molded by the Creator of the universe to fit perfectly into the big picture of creation. When the salmon fight their way up stream, and when the leaves go from green to gold and amber, they are doing precisely what they were designed to do. Do they understand this? Certainly not. Yet, one cannot help but look at the world and see "understanding" at work.

Try this: Look at a painting of a forest, a pear, or a child's face—and then look at a child. Do you see the presence of an artist? A molder?

Awesome, isn't it.

כֹּל אֲשֶׁר נִשְׁמָה בְּאַפּוֹ - **Everything that has [a neshama] the breath of life in its nostrils.** Apples and oranges are different, but not as different as rocks and oranges. Rocks don't grow, plants do. Trees and flowers are different, but not as different as trees and animals. Animals do more than just grow in one place, like plants do. Animals run, and fly, and hunt, and migrate. What about us? What makes us so different, so special? It's our soul.

God created rocks and trees and mountain goats, but He only "breathed the breath of life" into us. The Hebrew word for "breath," *neshima*, has the same root as *neshama*, which means "soul." When God "breathed" a soul into our bodies, He gave us freewill. Freewill, the ability to make thoughtful choices of consequence, is what makes us special. We use our freewill when we choose to do good, despite the hassle involved. We use our freewill when we choose to be responsible, regardless of what our friends may be doing. We use our freewill when we choose to ask the question, "What did God mold me for?" even when we suspect the answer might demand that we break out of a rut and strive for greatness.

719 AND COUNTING . . .

After decades of looking for the "right one," Marvin finally found Miriam. When their son was born, they named him Jacob, after Marvin's grandfather.

"My grandfather lived to be 103 and almost never missed a day of praying with a minyan in synagogue. After our son was born, I wanted to express my thanks to God, so I decided to make my own commitment to regularly attending a minyan. I've now gone 719 times without missing once. It's amazing how far a commitment can take you."

CHOOSE LIFE

עֲבוֹדָה - RESTORATION OF THE JERUSALEM TEMPLE

רְצֵה יהוה אֱלֹהֵינוּ בְּעַמְּךָ יִשְׂרָאֵל וּבִתְפִלָּתָם, וְהָשֵׁב אֶת הָעֲבוֹדָה לִדְבִיר בֵּיתֶךָ. וְאִשֵּׁי יִשְׂרָאֵל וּתְפִלָּתָם בְּאַהֲבָה תְקַבֵּל בְּרָצוֹן, וּתְהִי לְרָצוֹן תָּמִיד עֲבוֹדַת יִשְׂרָאֵל עַמֶּךָ.

וְתֶחֱזֶינָה עֵינֵינוּ בְּשׁוּבְךָ לְצִיּוֹן בְּרַחֲמִים. בָּרוּךְ אַתָּה יהוה, הַמַּחֲזִיר שְׁכִינָתוֹ לְצִיּוֹן.

→ *Amidah continues on page 132*

AVODAH
RESTORATION OF THE JERUSALEM TEMPLE SERVICE

Find pleasure, Adonai our God, with Your people Israel and their prayer, and restore the Temple service to the Holy of Holies in Your house, the Temple in Jerusalem. And accept Israel's fire-offerings, and their prayer, willingly, with love, and may You always find pleasure with the service of Israel, Your nation.

And let our eyes behold as You return to Zion, in compassionate mercy.

Blessed are You, Adonai, Who restores His Divine Presence to Zion.

→ *Amidah continues on page 133*

THE BIG PICTURE

We have now concluded the portion of the Amidah that is focused specifically on Rosh Hashanah. This paragraph begins the closing portion of our prayer.

We have prayed for everything—for ourselves and for the entire world. Now we pray for our prayers. Before we take leave of the King, we ask that He respond favorably to all we have requested, but we are not just asking for ourselves. We ask God to respond favorably to the prayers of every Jew on Rosh Hashanah. We ask God to look not only at us, but at every Jew everywhere.

There is a profound and transcendent connection that links all Jews together. In the spiritual realm, we are one. All of Israel shares a cosmic, collective soul. As individuals who are part of a trans-historical people—a meta-nation—we pray for one another's prayers. Deep in our souls, every Jew wants the same thing, and every Jewish soul is searching for the same thing: to blossom and flourish as a Jew. To see our people blossom and flourish. To be Jews, forever united as one, in our relationship to the ultimate *One*.

INSIGHTS

וְתֶחֱזֶינָה עֵינֵינוּ - And let our eyes behold. The Hebrew word *chozeh*, which means "behold," implies far more than just the ability to see. Chozeh means to see the world with the unfettered eyes of a visionary. A visionary sees as real what to others is just a dream. A visionary also detects depth and potential where others see the ordinary and the mundane.

This prayer says that we all have the ability to see life through the eyes of a visionary. We ask God to help us achieve that clear quality of perception because it is often possible for something profound to unfold right in front of us, and yet go completely unnoticed.

REFLECTION

As a child, when my mother would send me to look for something, I often came back to report that "It's not there." My mother's response? "Go look again, and this time, open your eyes." My mother is a very wise woman, and a bit of a visionary.

Somewhere right in front of you, there is a great opportunity. You may not have noticed yet, but it is there. Stop and look again, and again. Often, what we are looking for is not "out there somewhere," but rather, right here in front of us.

הוֹדָאָה - GRATITUDE TO GOD

(In the next paragraph, when you say the words We are grateful to You, *bow at the waist; for* A-donai, *straighten up and continue your prayer.)*

מוֹדִים אֲנַחְנוּ לָךְ שָׁאַתָּה הוּא יהוה אֱלֹהֵינוּ וֵאלֹהֵי אֲבוֹתֵינוּ לְעוֹלָם וָעֶד. צוּר חַיֵּינוּ, מָגֵן יִשְׁעֵנוּ אַתָּה הוּא לְדוֹר וָדוֹר. נוֹדֶה לְּךָ וּנְסַפֵּר תְּהִלָּתֶךָ עַל חַיֵּינוּ הַמְּסוּרִים בְּיָדֶךָ, וְעַל נִשְׁמוֹתֵינוּ הַפְּקוּדוֹת לָךְ, וְעַל נִסֶּיךָ שֶׁבְּכָל יוֹם עִמָּנוּ, וְעַל נִפְלְאוֹתֶיךָ וְטוֹבוֹתֶיךָ שֶׁבְּכָל עֵת, עֶרֶב וָבֹקֶר וְצָהֳרָיִם. הַטּוֹב כִּי לֹא כָלוּ רַחֲמֶיךָ, וְהַמְרַחֵם כִּי לֹא תַמּוּ חֲסָדֶיךָ, מֵעוֹלָם קִוִּינוּ לָךְ.

וְעַל כֻּלָּם יִתְבָּרַךְ וְיִתְרוֹמַם שִׁמְךָ מַלְכֵּנוּ תָּמִיד לְעוֹלָם וָעֶד.

וּכְתוֹב לְחַיִּים טוֹבִים כָּל בְּנֵי בְרִיתֶךָ.

(In the next paragraph, when you say the word Blessed, *bend your knees; for* You, *bow at the waist; for* A-donai, *straighten up and continue your prayer.)*

וְכֹל הַחַיִּים יוֹדוּךָ סֶּלָה, וִיהַלְלוּ אֶת שִׁמְךָ בֶּאֱמֶת, הָאֵל יְשׁוּעָתֵנוּ וְעֶזְרָתֵנוּ סֶלָה. בָּרוּךְ אַתָּה יהוה, הַטּוֹב שִׁמְךָ וּלְךָ נָאֶה לְהוֹדוֹת.

→ *Amidah continues on page 136*

HODA'AH - GRATITUDE TO GOD

(In the next paragraph, when you say the words We are grateful to You*, bow at the waist; for* A-donai*, straighten up and continue your prayer.)*

We are grateful to You, because it is You Adonai, Who for all eternity is our God and the God of our forefathers; You are the Rock of our lives and the Shield of our deliverance, from generation to generation.

We thank You and tell of Your praise, for our lives that are given over into Your hand—and for our souls that are in Your trusted care—and for Your miracles that accompany us every day, and for Your wonders and Your benevolence, at all times; evening, and morning and afternoon. You are the One Who is solely good, for Your compassion never ceases; and You are the One Who is solely compassionate, for Your kindness has never stopped; always have we placed our hope in You.

For all this, our King, may Your Name be blessed and extolled constantly and forever.

Inscribe for a good life . . .

And inscribe for a good life, all the children of Your covenant.

(In the next paragraph, when you say the word Blessed*, bend your knees; for* You*, bow at the waist; for* A-donai*, straighten up and continue your prayer.)*

And everything that is alive will express gratitude to You, forever; and sincerely praise Your Name, the all-powerful God of our salvation and help—forever.

Blessed are You, Adonai, "The Good, Benevolent One" is Your Name, and it is proper to express gratitude to You.

→ *Amidah continues on page 137*

THE BIG PICTURE

The Hebrew word for "thank you," *todah*, literally means "to admit." When we say "thank you," we are making an admission. We are admitting that we needed someone else, someone to pass the ketchup, help us in business, or raise us as a child. To say "thank you" means to admit that "I couldn't have done it without you." When we express our gratitude to a person or to God, we are recognizing our dependence and acknowledging the kind assistance we received. Though dependence is never easy to admit, when graciously acknowledged, it facilitates harmony, bonding, and relationship.

Gratitude is a character trait with the power to shape the rest of one's character, and much of one's life. Think of it this way: would you rather be friends with someone who is grateful, and who expresses their gratitude, or with an ingrate? Now there is a tough question for you. Nobody wants to be friends with an ingrate, nobody wants to marry an ingrate, and parents try very hard not to raise children who are ingrates. Why? Because ingrates naturally build walls, not bridges—between themselves and others, and themselves and God. Gratitude is the cornerstone of relationships.

INSIGHTS

לְעוֹלָם וָעֶד - Who for all eternity. People who have a family tree, especially one that stretches back more than a few generations, have a special perspective on history—and their place in it. Our roots in the past inform who we are today. As Jews, we have a family tree with roots that reach back over three millennia. Our relationship to God today is rooted in our forefathers' relationship to God—and this relationship is eternal. "For all eternity" and "from generation to generation;" we understand who we are today in the context of an unbroken chain of Jewish history, and an unbreakable bond with God. For this, and for all it implies, we are grateful: every year, every day, and every moment.

מֵעוֹלָם קִוִּינוּ לָךְ - Always have we placed our hope in You. As Jews, sometimes it's hard not to lose hope. I will never forget the following:

Malki Roth, aged 15, and her friend Michal Raziel, were having lunch at Sbarro in Jerusalem when a suicide bomber walked in and blew himself up. I visited the Roth family during the seven-day mourning period of *shiva*. Before I left the house, Arnold Roth, Malki's father, asked that I take two messages home with me—one from him, and one from Malki. He said, "Tell the Jews of America that we love it here. Tell them life is beautiful here. Tell them to come, to visit, to join us." And then he handed me a magazine article written by Malki in 1997. He told me he sensed that, through this article, Malki was speaking to all of us. He asked that I pay particular attention to the last paragraph. I did, and still do. This is what she wrote: "In conclusion, I want to say to all of you that are reading this right now: You are not allowed to lose your hope, because maybe a miracle will happen. DO NOT LOSE HOPE!"

REFLECTION

Most of us have someone in our life that we haven't thanked, or thanked sufficiently. A neighbor, colleague, teacher, co-worker, relative or spouse? Maybe a parent? Maybe God? Perhaps there is something inside holding us back. Perhaps we don't want to admit how needy we once were, or are? Well, it's time to get-over-it, and to say thank you. Thank you, thank you, and thank you—for all you have done for me.

⟡ שָׁלוֹם - PEACE ⟡

(During the morning Amidah prayer, say the paragraph on the right. In the afternoon and evening, say the paragraph on the left.)

(Morning Amidah)

שִׂים שָׁלוֹם, טוֹבָה וּבְרָכָה, חֵן וָחֶסֶד וְרַחֲמִים עָלֵינוּ וְעַל כָּל יִשְׂרָאֵל עַמֶּךָ. בָּרְכֵנוּ אָבִינוּ, כֻּלָּנוּ כְּאֶחָד בְּאוֹר פָּנֶיךָ, כִּי בְאוֹר פָּנֶיךָ נָתַתָּ לָּנוּ, יהוה אֱלֹהֵינוּ, תּוֹרַת חַיִּים וְאַהֲבַת חֶסֶד, וּצְדָקָה, וּבְרָכָה, וְרַחֲמִים, וְחַיִּים, וְשָׁלוֹם. וְטוֹב בְּעֵינֶיךָ לְבָרֵךְ אֶת עַמְּךָ יִשְׂרָאֵל, בְּכָל עֵת וּבְכָל שָׁעָה בִּשְׁלוֹמֶךָ.

(Afternoon and Evening Amidah)

שָׁלוֹם רָב עַל יִשְׂרָאֵל עַמְּךָ תָּשִׂים לְעוֹלָם, כִּי אַתָּה הוּא מֶלֶךְ אָדוֹן לְכָל הַשָּׁלוֹם. וְטוֹב בְּעֵינֶיךָ לְבָרֵךְ אֶת עַמְּךָ יִשְׂרָאֵל בְּכָל עֵת וּבְכָל שָׁעָה בִּשְׁלוֹמֶךָ.

SHALOM - PEACE

(During the morning Amidah prayer, say the paragraph on the left. In the afternoon and evening, say the paragraph on the right.)

(Morning Amidah)

Grant peace, goodness and blessing, favor, loving-kindness and compassion on us and on all the people of Israel, Your nation. Bless us, our Father, all of us together as one, with the spiritual light of Your Presence. For with the light of Your Presence You gave us, Adonai our God, the Torah of life and a love of kindness; moral integrity, blessing, compassion, life and peace. And may it be good in Your eyes to bless Your nation, the people of Israel, at all times and at every hour, with Your Peace.

(Afternoon and Evening Amidah)

Grant abundant peace on the people of Israel, Your nation—forever. For You are King, Master (and Director) of all peace. And may it be good in Your eyes to bless Your nation, the people of Israel, at all times and at every hour, with Your Peace.

בְּסֵפֶר חַיִּים בְּרָכָה וְשָׁלוֹם, וּפַרְנָסָה טוֹבָה, נִזָּכֵר וְנִכָּתֵב לְפָנֶיךָ,
אֲנַחְנוּ וְכָל עַמְּךָ בֵּית יִשְׂרָאֵל, לְחַיִּים טוֹבִים וּלְשָׁלוֹם.

(The next sentence concludes the paragraph of Shalom-Peace. There are two customs regarding the wording of this sentence. While both are acceptable, it is ideal to use the wording that is the custom in your synagogue.)

Version I

בָּרוּךְ אַתָּה יהוה, הַמְבָרֵךְ
אֶת עַמּוֹ יִשְׂרָאֵל בַּשָּׁלוֹם.

Version II

בָּרוּךְ אַתָּה יהוה,
עֹשֶׂה הַשָּׁלוֹם.

(There are also two customs regarding the next phrase. One custom is to say the phrase. The other omits it. While both are acceptable, it is ideal to follow the custom of your family or synagogue.)

יִהְיוּ לְרָצוֹן אִמְרֵי פִי וְהֶגְיוֹן לִבִּי לְפָנֶיךָ, יהוה צוּרִי וְגוֹאֲלִי.

→ *Amidah continues on page 142*

➻ IN THE BOOK OF LIFE . . .

In the book of life, blessing, peace and abundant livelihood, may we be remembered and inscribed before You; we and Your entire nation, the Family of Israel, for good life and for peace.

(The next sentence concludes the paragraph of Shalom-Peace. There are two customs regarding the wording of this sentence. While both are acceptable, it is ideal to use the wording that is the custom in your synagogue.)

Version I	**Version II**
Blessed are You, Adonai, Who blesses His nation, the people of Israel, with peace.	Blessed are You, Adonai, Who makes the peace.

(There are also two customs regarding the next phrase. One custom is to say the phrase. The other omits it. While both are acceptable, it is ideal to follow the custom of your family or synagogue.)

May the words of my mouth, and the thoughts of my heart, be favorably pleasant before You, Adonai, my Rock and my Redeemer.

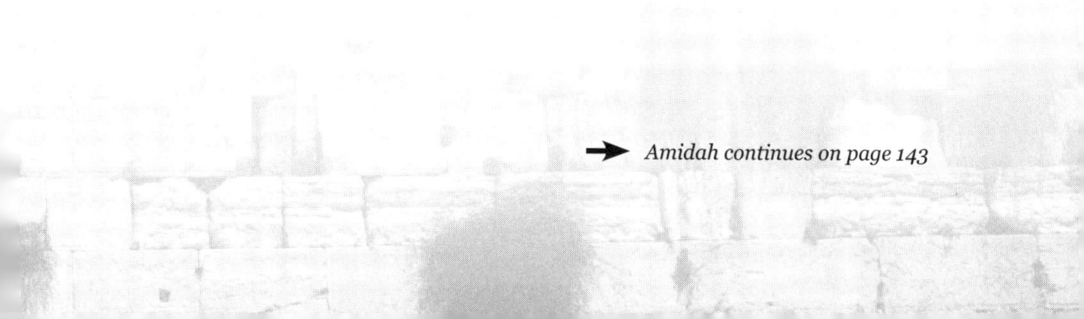

➔ *Amidah continues on page 143*

THE BIG PICTURE

The Hebrew word for "peace," *shalom*, literally means "whole" or "complete." We are accustomed to thinking of peace as being the absence of hostility, but the word *shalom* means far more than that. *Shalom* means absolute, pristine harmony. *Shalom* is present when every instrument in an orchestra is perfectly integrated with the others, when every player on a team is working in precise unison, and when a husband and wife are lovingly devoted to the actualization of one another's individual potential, as well as their shared potential.

Our sages taught that "The perfect container for blessing, is peace." When there is peace between business partners, then it's far more likely the business will flourish. When there is peace between a husband and wife, then all the blessings in their life will feel much richer. When there is peace between people, and between nations, the world's blessings will reveal themselves like never before.

At the conclusion of every Amidah—weekday, Shabbat, and holidays—we pray for peace. Without peace, all the blessings in the world, and all the answered prayers, are at risk of slipping through our fingers. With peace, the possibility for blessing is almost endless.

INSIGHTS

בְּאוֹר פָּנֶיךָ - Spiritual light of Your Presence. The Kabbalah uses "light" as a metaphor for God's Presence. In kabbalah, the epiphany of creation is termed, *ohr aiyn sof*, which means, the appearance of God's "endless light." This "light" is not to be confused with the kind of light that comes from flashlights and stars: it's not the kind of light that dispels darkness. Rather, the original "light" of creation is a reference to God being "present" in creation in a way that we can relate to. The expression, and manifestation of God in creation—the Divine Presence that we can connect with—is called "light."

Without light, life is not possible. The same is true of God's "light," without it, there is no possibility of life. The "light" of God is what makes existence not only possible, but meaningful. More than just sustain life, God's "light" is what elevates life; it's what creates the possibility for spirituality, and, it's what places a relationship with God within the reach of every human being.

תּוֹרַת חַיִּים - Torah of life. The Hebrew words for "Torah of life" can also be translated as "instructions for living." One of the most valuable gifts parents can give their children is sound wisdom. With sound wisdom; with an appreciation of what is important in life and what isn't; with an awareness of what fills life with meaning and what doesn't; and with an understanding of how to build relationships and not undermine them—a person has many of the essential tools for life. The Torah that God gave to the Jewish people contains history, commandments, ethics, stories, and more—and all of these have one element in common—they are wellsprings of indispensable wisdom for life.

REFLECTION

A love of kindness.

We can all say this: "Somewhere in my life there is an opportunity for kindness; to listen to a friend who needs to talk, to help someone in need, or perhaps to encourage a struggling colleague." The hallmark of the life of Abraham and Sarah—the first Jews—was their devotion to kindness, no matter who the beneficiary was. We have inherited that devotion, that "love of kindness"—it's part of our spiritual DNA. To be kind is to be true to yourself.

אֱלֹהַי, נְצוֹר לְשׁוֹנִי מֵרָע, וּשְׂפָתַי מִדַּבֵּר מִרְמָה, וְלִמְקַלְלַי נַפְשִׁי תִדּוֹם, וְנַפְשִׁי כֶּעָפָר לַכֹּל תִּהְיֶה. פְּתַח לִבִּי בְּתוֹרָתֶךָ, וּבְמִצְוֹתֶיךָ תִּרְדּוֹף נַפְשִׁי. וְכֹל הַחוֹשְׁבִים עָלַי רָעָה, מְהֵרָה הָפֵר עֲצָתָם וְקַלְקֵל מַחֲשַׁבְתָּם. עֲשֵׂה לְמַעַן שְׁמֶךָ, עֲשֵׂה לְמַעַן יְמִינֶךָ, עֲשֵׂה לְמַעַן קְדֻשָּׁתֶךָ, עֲשֵׂה לְמַעַן תּוֹרָתֶךָ. לְמַעַן יֵחָלְצוּן יְדִידֶיךָ, הוֹשִׁיעָה יְמִינְךָ וַעֲנֵנִי. יִהְיוּ לְרָצוֹן אִמְרֵי פִי וְהֶגְיוֹן לִבִּי לְפָנֶיךָ, יהוה צוּרִי וְגוֹאֲלִי.

(As you begin the next phrase, bow slightly and take three steps back. When you say the words He who makes peace, *bow to your left; for* may He make peace, *bow to your right; for* And upon all Israel . . . *bow forward.)*

(Bow slightly and take three steps back—)

(Bow to your left) עֹשֶׂה [הַ]שָּׁלוֹם בִּמְרוֹמָיו,

(Bow to your right) הוּא יַעֲשֶׂה שָׁלוֹם עָלֵינוּ,

(Bow forward) וְעַל כָּל יִשְׂרָאֵל. וְאִמְרוּ: אָמֵן.

➔ *Amidah continues on page 146*

THE AMIDAH CONCLUDES WITH THIS PARAGRAPH

My God, guard my tongue from evil and my lips from speaking deceitfully. And towards those who curse me, may my soul not respond; and let my soul be (humble) like dust towards everyone. Open my heart to Your Torah and enable my soul to passionately pursue Your commandments. And for all those who plan evil designs against me, quickly void their plots and undermine their intentions. Do this (please) for the sake of Your Name. Do this (please) for the sake of Your right hand. (So that Your Divine involvement in life will be clear to all.) Do this (please) for the sake of (restoring awareness of) Your Holiness. Do this (please) for the sake of (restoring honor to) Your Torah. So that Your beloved (nation) will be freed (from their suffering and oppression)—May Your right hand deliver salvation, and answer me.

May the words of my mouth, and the thoughts of my heart, be favorably pleasant before You, Adonai, my Rock and my Redeemer.

(As you begin the next phrase, bow slightly and take three steps back. When you say the words He who makes peace, *bow to your left; for* may He make peace, *bow to your right; for* And upon all Israel . . . *bow forward.)*

(Bow slightly and take three steps back—)

(Bow to your left)	He Who makes peace in His highest realms,
(Bow to your right)	May He make peace upon us,
(Bow forward)	And upon all the people of Israel, and say, amen.

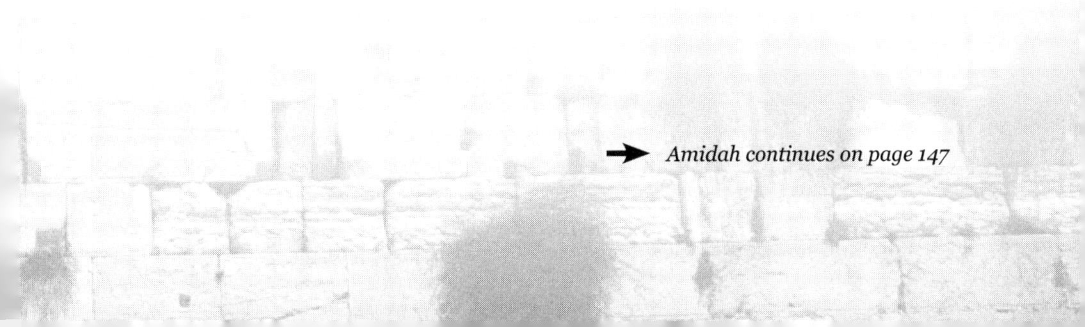

→ *Amidah continues on page 147*

THE BIG PICTURE

As a rule, most endeavors are only as successful as the preparation one puts into them. Jewish life is brimming with rich, spiritual endeavors. Holidays, commandments, observances, and the Amidah: each is brimming with potential. Our sages taught that to access the full potential in Jewish life, we need to pay close attention to how we prepare for events, and how we depart. Conscious preparation focuses our mind, heart, and soul. Conscious departure enables us to gather the harvest of our experience, bundle it up, and take it home.

Way back at the beginning of the Amidah, there was a short phrase that helped us focus: "God, my Master, open my lips so that my mouth will tell of Your praise." Now, as we take leave of the Amidah—of our intimate encounter with God—we do so with this final paragraph. We say: "My God, guard my tongue from evil and my lips from speaking deceitfully." Prayer is simply, and profoundly, the opportunity to speak to God—and speech is remarkable. We open our lips, emit sound waves, and are able to express what is in our minds, hearts, and souls. Speech is the instrument through which we reach out and connect to others, and to God. Speech goes to the heart of what makes us holy.

As you are about to step away from the Amidah, make sure you don't leave God behind. Would you like to know a secret for maintaining an awareness of being in God's Presence? Treat your lips like they are holy: speak honestly, speak with kindness, and speak like you are a guest in the king's inner sanctum—because you are.

INSIGHTS

וְנַפְשִׁי כֶּעָפָר - Let my soul be humble like dust. You will recall (at least I hope you will), that the day on which the first human being was created was Rosh Hashanah, and that, in a sense, we are all that first person. In relation to the vast cosmos, what are we if not mere specs of dust? And what is our life, if not the tiniest blip in eons of time?

On page 15, we saw that the first human being was created "from the dust of the earth." We also saw that the world into which he was created was completely barren and covered with nothing but dust. A "dusty" man in a "dusty" world—yet both possessed near limitless potential. To view ourselves "like dust" is to see what we truly are: little nothings, capable of partnering with God, in the perfection of everything.

REFLECTION

Do any of the following statements sound familiar to you? "I know today is Rosh Hashanah, but I just don't feel inspired." "I've tried doing some Jewish stuff, but it just doesn't do anything for me." "Yeah, I'm Jewish, but I don't feel any special connection to other Jews, or to Israel." Feeling emotionally connected to your Judaism is important, but it's not everything. In fact, it's certainly possible, and even common, to pray the entire Amidah and still not feel anything. Think of it this way: In baseball, if a batter gets just three hits out of every ten attempts, he's a star.

It is critical for you to know that every effort you make to connect to Judaism, to who you are deep inside, to Rosh Hashanah, and to God, is exceptionally meaningful. Unlike baseball, in Judaism, even if you don't "get a hit," the effort alone produces enduring spiritual growth. If you aren't feeling anything, don't give up, eventually the feelings will come. However, if you would rather not wait, well, there is a short cut—just turn to God and ask: "Open my heart to Your Torah and enable my soul to passionately pursue Your commandments." Go ahead—ask.

And by the way; if today is Rosh Hashanah, and you are reading this book or have just completed the Amidah, then your heart already is open.

יְהִי רָצוֹן מִלְּפָנֶיךָ, יהוה אֱלֹהֵינוּ וֵאלֹהֵי אֲבוֹתֵינוּ, שֶׁיִּבָּנֶה בֵּית
: הַמִּקְדָּשׁ בִּמְהֵרָה בְיָמֵינוּ, וְתֵן חֶלְקֵנוּ בְּתוֹרָתֶךָ, וְשָׁם נַעֲבָדְךָ
בְּיִרְאָה, כִּימֵי עוֹלָם וּכְשָׁנִים קַדְמוֹנִיּוֹת. וְעָרְבָה לַיהוה מִנְחַת
יְהוּדָה וִירוּשָׁלָיִם, כִּימֵי עוֹלָם וּכְשָׁנִים קַדְמוֹנִיּוֹת.

✧ Closing meditation

When the Jewish nation finally returns home; when Jerusalem and the Temple are rebuilt, when every Jew achieves a sense of personal connection to the Torah—God's instructions for life—and when every Jew has a deep relationship with the Creator, then everything else will fall into place: for us and for the entire world.

With the three steps we took back, we were stepping out of a rarefied dimension of God consciousness, a place where we were literally able to speak to God. Following the closing meditation paragraph, for a few moments, remain standing—still and silent. Let the experience of the Amidah settle into your being, and take it with you—forever.

May it be Your will, Adonai, our God and God of our forefathers, that the holy Temple be rebuilt, speedily in our days; And grant us our personal share in Your Torah, and we will serve You there with reverence, as in the days of antiquity, and in earlier years. Then the offerings of (the people of) Judah and Jerusalem will be pleasantly acceptable to God, as in the days of antiquity, and in earlier years.

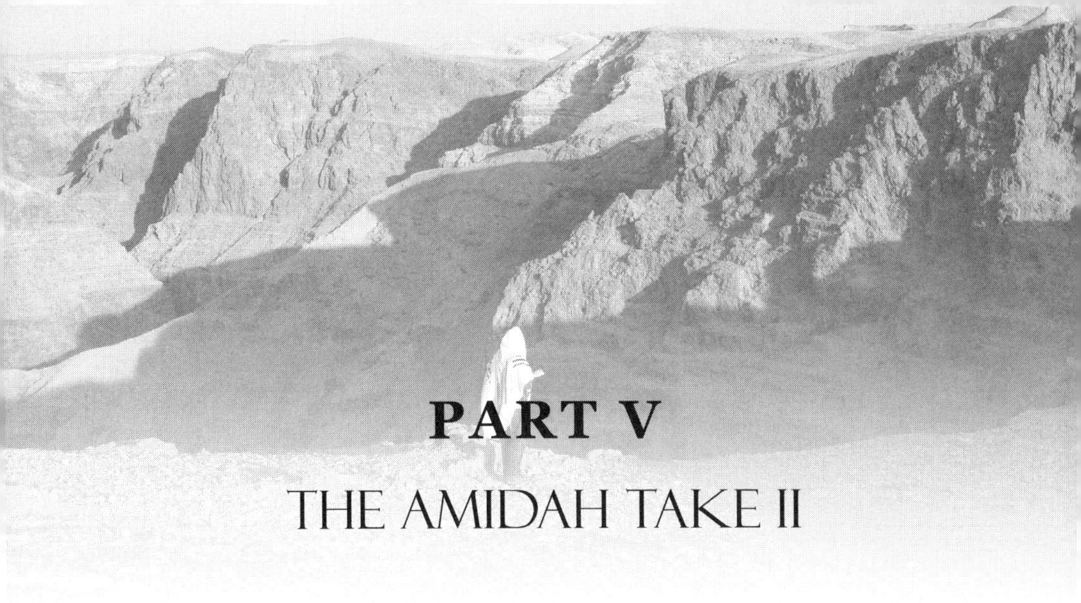

PART V

THE AMIDAH TAKE II

For some people, insights and explanations in a prayer book can be distracting. For those of you who prefer to concentrate only on the words, this is the Amidah for you.

(Take three steps backward, then three steps forward: now, it's just you and God.)

אֲדֹנָי שְׂפָתַי תִּפְתָּח וּפִי יַגִּיד תְּהִלָּתֶךָ.

⇝ אָבוֹת - FOREFATHERS ⇜

(When you say the word Blessed, *bend your knees; for* You, *bow at the waist; for* A-donai, *straighten up and continue your prayer while standing.)*

בָּרוּךְ אַתָּה יהוה אֱלֹהֵינוּ וֵאלֹהֵי אֲבוֹתֵינוּ, אֱלֹהֵי אַבְרָהָם,
ד אֱלֹהֵי יִצְחָק, וֵאלֹהֵי יַעֲקֹב, הָאֵל הַגָּדוֹל הַגִּבּוֹר וְהַנּוֹרָא, אֵל
עֶלְיוֹן, גּוֹמֵל חֲסָדִים טוֹבִים וְקֹנֵה הַכֹּל, וְזוֹכֵר חַסְדֵי אָבוֹת,
וּמֵבִיא גוֹאֵל לִבְנֵי בְנֵיהֶם, לְמַעַן שְׁמוֹ בְּאַהֲבָה.

זָכְרֵנוּ לְחַיִּים, מֶלֶךְ חָפֵץ בַּחַיִּים, וְכָתְבֵנוּ בְּסֵפֶר הַחַיִּים, לְמַעַנְךָ
אֱלֹהִים חַיִּים.

(When you say the word Blessed, *bend your knees; for* You, *bow at the waist; for* A-donai, *straighten up and continue your prayer while standing.)*

מֶלֶךְ עוֹזֵר וּמוֹשִׁיעַ וּמָגֵן. בָּרוּךְ אַתָּה יהוה, מָגֵן אַבְרָהָם.

✤ Request for assistance, even in prayer

(Take three steps backward, then three steps forward: now, it's just you and God.)

Adonai, my Master, open my lips so that my mouth will tell of Your praise.

✤ The Amidah begins . . .

✤ AVOT - FOREFATHERS ✤

(When you say the word Blessed, *bend your knees; for* You, *bow at the waist; for* A-donai, *straighten up and continue your prayer while standing.)*

Blessed are You, Adonai, our God and God of our forefathers; God of Avraham, (Abraham) God of Yitzchak, (Isaac) and God of Yacov (Jacob):

The (God Who is the only true, ultimate) Power, *the* Great, *the* Mighty, and *the* Awesome—God Most High, Who bestows good, loving kindness and owns everything, and remembers the kind actions of the Forefathers, and brings a redeemer to their children's children, for the sake of His Name, out of love.

✤ Remember us for life

Remember us for life, King Who desires life, and inscribe us into the Book of Life—for Your sake—Living God.

(When you say the word Blessed, *bend your knees; for* You, *bow at the waist; for* A-donai, *straighten up and continue your prayer while standing.)*

King, Helper and Savior and Shield. Blessed are You Adonai, Shield of Avraham, (Abraham).

גְּבוּרוֹת - POWERS

אַתָּה גִּבּוֹר לְעוֹלָם אֲדֹנָי, מְחַיֵּה מֵתִים אַתָּה, רַב לְהוֹשִׁיעַ. - מְכַלְכֵּל חַיִּים בְּחֶסֶד, מְחַיֵּה מֵתִים בְּרַחֲמִים רַבִּים, סוֹמֵךְ נוֹפְלִים, וְרוֹפֵא חוֹלִים, וּמַתִּיר אֲסוּרִים, וּמְקַיֵּם אֱמוּנָתוֹ לִישֵׁנֵי עָפָר. מִי כָמוֹךָ בַּעַל גְּבוּרוֹת, וּמִי דּוֹמֶה לָּךְ, מֶלֶךְ מֵמִית וּמְחַיֶּה וּמַצְמִיחַ יְשׁוּעָה.

מִי כָמוֹךָ אַב הָרַחֲמִים, זוֹכֵר יְצוּרָיו לְחַיִּים בְּרַחֲמִים.

וְנֶאֱמָן אַתָּה לְהַחֲיוֹת מֵתִים. בָּרוּךְ אַתָּה יהוה, מְחַיֵּה הַמֵּתִים.

GEVUROT - POWERS

You are eternally Powerful, my Master,

You are the Reviver of the dead, completely able to save us.

The one Who Sustains the living with loving-kindness,

Reviver of the dead with Your greatly abundant mercy.

The one Who Supports those who have fallen, Who is the Healer of the sick,

Who frees the imprisoned, and upholds His faithfulness to those asleep in the dust.

Who is like You, Master of all powers, and who resembles You, a King Who causes death and restores life, and causes salvation to sprout.

WHO IS LIKE YOU?

Who is like You, merciful Father, Who mercifully remembers His creations—for life.

And You are faithful to revive the dead. Blessed are You, Adonai, Who revives the dead.

קְדוּשַּׁת הַשֵּׁם - SANCTITY OF GOD'S NAME

אַתָּה קָדוֹשׁ וְשִׁמְךָ קָדוֹשׁ, וּקְדוֹשִׁים בְּכָל יוֹם יְהַלְלוּךָ סֶּלָה.

וּבְכֵן, תֵּן פַּחְדְּךָ, יהוה אֱלֹהֵינוּ, עַל כָּל מַעֲשֶׂיךָ, וְאֵימָתְךָ עַל כָּל מַה שֶּׁבָּרָאתָ. וְיִירָאוּךָ כָּל הַמַּעֲשִׂים, וְיִשְׁתַּחֲווּ לְפָנֶיךָ כָּל הַבְּרוּאִים. וְיֵעָשׂוּ כֻלָּם אֲגֻדָּה אַחַת, לַעֲשׂוֹת רְצוֹנְךָ בְּלֵבָב שָׁלֵם. כְּמוֹ שֶׁיָּדַעְנוּ, יהוה אֱלֹהֵינוּ, שֶׁהַשָּׁלְטָן לְפָנֶיךָ, עֹז בְּיָדְךָ, וּגְבוּרָה בִּימִינֶךָ, וְשִׁמְךָ נוֹרָא עַל כָּל מַה שֶּׁבָּרָאתָ.

וּבְכֵן, תֵּן כָּבוֹד, יהוה, לְעַמֶּךָ, תְּהִלָּה לִירֵאֶיךָ, וְתִקְוָה טוֹבָה לְדוֹרְשֶׁיךָ, וּפִתְחוֹן פֶּה לַמְיַחֲלִים לָךְ, שִׂמְחָה לְאַרְצֶךָ, וְשָׂשׂוֹן לְעִירֶךָ, וּצְמִיחַת קֶרֶן לְדָוִד עַבְדֶּךָ, וַעֲרִיכַת נֵר לְבֶן יִשַׁי מְשִׁיחֶךָ, בִּמְהֵרָה בְיָמֵינוּ.

KEDUSHAT HASHEM - SANCTITY OF GOD'S NAME

You are holy and Your Name is holy, and holy ones praise You daily—forever.

And therefore, place your dread . . .

And therefore, place your dread, Adonai our God, on all Your works,

And Your awe on all You have created.

And then all Your works will fear You, and all Your created beings will prostrate themselves before You. Enable them all to form a single society, to carry out Your will with a complete heart.

For as we know, Adonai our God, that rulership is Yours alone, might is in Your hand and power is in Your right hand, and Your awe-inspiring Name is upon all You have created.

And also, then, grant honor . . .

And also, then, grant honor, Adonai, to Your nation, praise to those who fear You, and good hope to those who are searching for You, and an open mouth to those who yearn for You:

Joy to Your land and rejoicing to Your city; a proud, sprouting shoot to David Your servant, and a prepared light for the son of Yishai (Jesse), Your anointed, speedily in our days.

וּבְכֵן, צַדִּיקִים יִרְאוּ וְיִשְׂמָחוּ, וִישָׁרִים יַעֲלֹזוּ, וַחֲסִידִים בְּרִנָּה יָגִילוּ. וְעוֹלָתָה תִּקְפָּץ פִּיהָ, וְכָל הָרִשְׁעָה כֻּלָּהּ כְּעָשָׁן תִּכְלֶה, כִּי תַעֲבִיר מֶמְשֶׁלֶת זָדוֹן מִן הָאָרֶץ.

וְתִמְלוֹךְ, אַתָּה יהוה לְבַדֶּךָ, עַל כָּל מַעֲשֶׂיךָ, בְּהַר צִיּוֹן מִשְׁכַּן כְּבוֹדֶךָ, וּבִירוּשָׁלַיִם עִיר קָדְשֶׁךָ, כַּכָּתוּב בְּדִבְרֵי קָדְשֶׁךָ: יִמְלֹךְ יהוה לְעוֹלָם, אֱלֹהַיִךְ צִיּוֹן לְדֹר וָדֹר, הַלְלוּיָהּ.

קָדוֹשׁ אַתָּה וְנוֹרָא שְׁמֶךָ, וְאֵין אֱלוֹהַּ מִבַּלְעָדֶיךָ, כַּכָּתוּב: וַיִּגְבַּהּ יהוה צְבָאוֹת בַּמִּשְׁפָּט, וְהָאֵל הַקָּדוֹשׁ נִקְדַּשׁ בִּצְדָקָה. בָּרוּךְ אַתָּה יהוה, הַמֶּלֶךְ הַקָּדוֹשׁ.

And also, then, the righteous . . .

And also, then, the righteous will see (this world) and rejoice, the straight will exult, and the devout will express their jubilance with song.

Injustice will shut its mouth and all wickedness will vanish like smoke, when You remove tyrannical regimes from the earth.

And then You alone will reign . . .

And then You alone, Adonai, will reign over all Your works, on Mount Zion, dwelling place of Your Presence; and in Jerusalem, Your holy city, as it is written in Your holy words: "Adonai will reign forever—Zion, Your God—from generation to generation. Praise God."

Holy is what You are . . .

Holy is what You are; and Your Name is awesome, and there is no god other than You, as it is written: "Adonai, Master of all heavenly creations, through Your judgment of the world You will be exalted, and the Almighty Holy One, through righteousness You will be sanctified."

Blessed are You, Adonai, the King who is the Holy One.

קְדוּשַּׁת הַיּוֹם - SANCTITY OF THE DAY

אַתָּה בְחַרְתָּנוּ מִכָּל הָעַמִּים, אָהַבְתָּ אוֹתָנוּ, וְרָצִיתָ בָּנוּ, וְרוֹמַמְתָּנוּ מִכָּל הַלְּשׁוֹנוֹת, וְקִדַּשְׁתָּנוּ בְּמִצְוֹתֶיךָ. וְקֵרַבְתָּנוּ מַלְכֵּנוּ לַעֲבוֹדָתֶךָ, וְשִׁמְךָ הַגָּדוֹל וְהַקָּדוֹשׁ עָלֵינוּ קָרָאתָ.

(On Saturday night only, add the following paragraph. On all other nights, continue to the next paragraph.)

וַתּוֹדִיעֵנוּ יהוה אֱלֹהֵינוּ אֶת מִשְׁפְּטֵי צִדְקֶךָ, וַתְּלַמְּדֵנוּ לַעֲשׂוֹת (בָּהֶם) חֻקֵּי רְצוֹנֶךָ. וַתִּתֶּן לָנוּ יהוה אֱלֹהֵינוּ מִשְׁפָּטִים יְשָׁרִים וְתוֹרוֹת אֱמֶת חֻקִּים וּמִצְוֹת טוֹבִים. וַתַּנְחִילֵנוּ זְמַנֵּי שָׂשׂוֹן וּמוֹעֲדֵי קֹדֶשׁ וְחַגֵּי נְדָבָה. וַתּוֹרִישֵׁנוּ קְדֻשַּׁת שַׁבָּת וּכְבוֹד מוֹעֵד וַחֲגִיגַת הָרֶגֶל. וַתַּבְדֵּל יהוה אֱלֹהֵינוּ בֵּין קֹדֶשׁ לְחוֹל, בֵּין אוֹר לְחֹשֶׁךְ, בֵּין יִשְׂרָאֵל לָעַמִּים, בֵּין יוֹם הַשְּׁבִיעִי לְשֵׁשֶׁת יְמֵי הַמַּעֲשֶׂה. בֵּין קְדֻשַּׁת שַׁבָּת לִקְדֻשַּׁת יוֹם טוֹב הִבְדַּלְתָּ, וְאֶת יוֹם הַשְּׁבִיעִי מִשֵּׁשֶׁת יְמֵי הַמַּעֲשֶׂה קִדַּשְׁתָּ, הִבְדַּלְתָּ וְקִדַּשְׁתָּ אֶת עַמְּךָ יִשְׂרָאֵל בִּקְדֻשָּׁתֶךָ.

(On Shabbat, add the words in brackets.)

וַתִּתֶּן לָנוּ יהוה אֱלֹהֵינוּ בְּאַהֲבָה אֶת יוֹם [הַשַּׁבָּת הַזֶּה וְאֶת יוֹם] הַזִּכָּרוֹן הַזֶּה, יוֹם [זִכְרוֹן] תְּרוּעָה [בְּאַהֲבָה] מִקְרָא קֹדֶשׁ, זֵכֶר לִיצִיאַת מִצְרָיִם.

KEDUSHAT HAYOM - SANCTITY OF THE DAY

You have chosen us from among all the nations. You loved us and took pleasure in us.

You elevated us above all the other languages and you made us holy through your commandments. You drew us close, Our King, to Your service, and You have associated Your great and holy name with us.

(On Saturday night only, add the following two paragraphs. On all other nights, continue to the next paragraph.)

You made known to us, Adonai, our God, Your righteous laws, and You have taught us to do the edicts of Your will. And You gave us, Adonai our God, just and equitable laws and teachings of truth, good edicts and commandments. You gave us as a heritage, seasons of rejoicing, appointed holidays of holiness and the voluntary offerings of the festivals. And You bequeathed to us the holiness of Shabbat, the weighty significance of the appointed holiday and the celebration of the festival.

And You distinguished, Adonai our God, between the holy and the mundane, between light and darkness, between Israel and the other nations, between the seventh day and the six days of work. Between the (special) holiness of Shabbat and the holiness of the holiday You have distinguished. And the seventh day, from amidst the six work days, You have made holy. You designated and invested with holiness—Your nation Israel—with Your holiness.

(On Shabbat, add the words in brackets.)

And You gave us, Adonai our God, out of love, [this Shabbat day and] this Day of Remembering, a day for [the remembrance of] sounding the shofar [out of love] a day designated by holiness—commemorating the Exodus from Egypt.

אֱלֹהֵינוּ וֵאלֹהֵי אֲבוֹתֵינוּ, יַעֲלֶה, וְיָבֹא, וְיַגִּיעַ, וְיֵרָאֶה, וְיֵרָצֶה, וְיִשָּׁמַע, וְיִפָּקֵד, וְיִזָּכֵר זִכְרוֹנֵנוּ וּפִקְדוֹנֵנוּ, וְזִכְרוֹן אֲבוֹתֵינוּ, וְזִכְרוֹן מָשִׁיחַ בֶּן דָּוִד עַבְדֶּךָ, וְזִכְרוֹן יְרוּשָׁלַיִם עִיר קָדְשֶׁךָ, וְזִכְרוֹן כָּל עַמְּךָ בֵּית יִשְׂרָאֵל לְפָנֶיךָ, לִפְלֵיטָה לְטוֹבָה לְחֵן וּלְחֶסֶד וּלְרַחֲמִים, לְחַיִּים וּלְשָׁלוֹם בְּיוֹם הַזִּכָּרוֹן הַזֶּה. זָכְרֵנוּ יהוה אֱלֹהֵינוּ בּוֹ לְטוֹבָה, וּפָקְדֵנוּ בוֹ לִבְרָכָה, וְהוֹשִׁיעֵנוּ בוֹ לְחַיִּים. וּבִדְבַר יְשׁוּעָה וְרַחֲמִים, חוּס וְחָנֵּנוּ וְרַחֵם עָלֵינוּ וְהוֹשִׁיעֵנוּ, כִּי אֵלֶיךָ עֵינֵינוּ, כִּי אֵל מֶלֶךְ חַנּוּן וְרַחוּם אָתָּה.

May there ascend, come and arrive . . .

Our God and God of our forefathers, allow there to ascend, come and arrive; and appear, be accepted and heard, be counted and remembered—our remembrance and our being noticed and counted—and the remembrance of our forefathers, and the remembrance of the Messiah, the son of David, Your servant; and the remembrance of Jerusalem Your holy city and the remembrance of Your entire nation , the Family of Israel, before You—for deliverance, well-being, favor, kindness and mercy; for life and peace on this Day of Remembering.

Remember us, Adonai our God, today, for goodness, and pay close attention to us, today, for blessing, and rescue us, today, for life. In keeping with the promise of deliverance and mercy, spare us and be pleased with us, have compassion on us and rescue us; for our eyes are turned in hope to You, because You are God, the gracious and merciful King.

אֱלֹהֵינוּ וֵאלֹהֵי אֲבוֹתֵינוּ, מְלוֹךְ עַל כָּל הָעוֹלָם כֻּלּוֹ בִּכְבוֹדֶךָ, וְהִנָּשֵׂא עַל כָּל הָאָרֶץ בִּיקָרֶךָ, וְהוֹפַע בַּהֲדַר גְּאוֹן עֻזֶּךָ, עַל כָּל יוֹשְׁבֵי תֵבֵל אַרְצֶךָ. וְיֵדַע כָּל פָּעוּל כִּי אַתָּה פְעַלְתּוֹ, וְיָבִין כָּל יָצוּר כִּי אַתָּה יְצַרְתּוֹ, וְיֹאמַר כֹּל אֲשֶׁר נְשָׁמָה בְאַפּוֹ, יהוה אֱלֹהֵי יִשְׂרָאֵל מֶלֶךְ, וּמַלְכוּתוֹ בַּכֹּל מָשָׁלָה.

(On Shabbat, add the words in brackets)

[אֱלֹהֵינוּ וֵאלֹהֵי אֲבוֹתֵינוּ, רְצֵה בִמְנוּחָתֵנוּ] קַדְּשֵׁנוּ בְּמִצְוֹתֶיךָ, וְתֵן חֶלְקֵנוּ בְּתוֹרָתֶךָ, שַׂבְּעֵנוּ מִטּוּבֶךָ, וְשַׂמְּחֵנוּ בִּישׁוּעָתֶךָ. [וְהַנְחִילֵנוּ, יהוה אֱלֹהֵינוּ, בְּאַהֲבָה וּבְרָצוֹן שַׁבַּת קָדְשֶׁךָ, וְיָנוּחוּ בָהּ יִשְׂרָאֵל מְקַדְּשֵׁי שְׁמֶךָ.] וְטַהֵר לִבֵּנוּ לְעָבְדְּךָ בֶּאֱמֶת. כִּי אַתָּה אֱלֹהִים אֱמֶת, וּדְבָרְךָ אֱמֶת וְקַיָּם לָעַד. בָּרוּךְ אַתָּה יהוה, מֶלֶךְ עַל כָּל הָאָרֶץ, מְקַדֵּשׁ [הַשַּׁבָּת וְ] יִשְׂרָאֵל וְיוֹם הַזִּכָּרוֹן.

❖ Reign over the entire universe . . .

Our God and God of our forefathers, reign over the entire universe, in Your esteemed honor; and be elevated over the entire earth in Your grandeur, and let Your eminence shine in the brilliance of Your majestic power over all who live in the settled regions of Your earth. So that everything that was made will know that You made it, and everything that was molded will understand that You molded it, and everything that has the breath of life (the soul) in its nostrils will say: "Adonai, God of Israel is King, and His kingdom reigns over everything."

(On Shabbat, add the words in brackets)

[Our God and God of our forefathers, be pleased with our rest] Make us holy through Your commandments and give us our unique portion in Your Torah; satisfy us from Your goodness and make us joyous in Your deliverance. [And give us our heritage Adonai, our God, with love and favor, Your holy Shabbat, and may Israel—the nation that sanctifies Your Name—rest on it.] And purify our hearts to serve You with true integrity, for You God are truth and Your word is true and endures forever.

Blessed are You, Adonai, King over the entire earth, Who sanctifies [the Shabbat and] Israel and the Day of Remembering.

✦ עֲבוֹדָה - RESTORATION OF THE JERUSALEM TEMPLE ✦

רְצֵה יהוה אֱלֹהֵינוּ בְּעַמְּךָ יִשְׂרָאֵל וּבִתְפִלָּתָם, וְהָשֵׁב אֶת הָעֲבוֹדָה לִדְבִיר בֵּיתֶךָ. וְאִשֵּׁי יִשְׂרָאֵל וּתְפִלָּתָם בְּאַהֲבָה תְקַבֵּל בְּרָצוֹן, וּתְהִי לְרָצוֹן תָּמִיד עֲבוֹדַת יִשְׂרָאֵל עַמֶּךָ.

וְתֶחֱזֶינָה עֵינֵינוּ בְּשׁוּבְךָ לְצִיּוֹן בְּרַחֲמִים. בָּרוּךְ אַתָּה יהוה, הַמַּחֲזִיר שְׁכִינָתוֹ לְצִיּוֹן.

AVODAH
RESTORATION OF THE JERUSALEM TEMPLE SERVICE

Find pleasure, Adonai our God, with Your people Israel and their prayer, and restore the Temple service to the Holy of Holies in Your house, the Temple in Jerusalem. And accept Israel's fire-offerings, and their prayer, willingly, with love, and may You always find pleasure with the service of Israel, Your nation.

And let our eyes behold as You return to Zion, in compassionate mercy.

Blessed are You, Adonai, Who restores His Divine Presence to Zion.

הוֹדָאָה - GRATITUDE TO GOD

(In the next paragraph, when you say the words We are grateful to You, *bow at the waist; for* A-donai, *straighten up and continue your prayer.)*

מוֹדִים אֲנַחְנוּ לָךְ שָׁאַתָּה הוּא יהוה אֱלֹהֵינוּ וֵאלֹהֵי אֲבוֹתֵינוּ לְעוֹלָם וָעֶד. צוּר חַיֵּינוּ, מָגֵן יִשְׁעֵנוּ אַתָּה הוּא לְדוֹר וָדוֹר. נוֹדֶה לְךָ וּנְסַפֵּר תְּהִלָּתֶךָ עַל חַיֵּינוּ הַמְּסוּרִים בְּיָדֶךָ, וְעַל נִשְׁמוֹתֵינוּ הַפְּקוּדוֹת לָךְ, וְעַל נִסֶּיךָ שֶׁבְּכָל יוֹם עִמָּנוּ, וְעַל נִפְלְאוֹתֶיךָ וְטוֹבוֹתֶיךָ שֶׁבְּכָל עֵת, עֶרֶב וָבֹקֶר וְצָהֳרָיִם. הַטּוֹב כִּי לֹא כָלוּ רַחֲמֶיךָ, וְהַמְרַחֵם כִּי לֹא תַמּוּ חֲסָדֶיךָ, מֵעוֹלָם קִוִּינוּ לָךְ.

וְעַל כֻּלָּם יִתְבָּרַךְ וְיִתְרוֹמַם שִׁמְךָ מַלְכֵּנוּ תָּמִיד לְעוֹלָם וָעֶד.

וּכְתוֹב לְחַיִּים טוֹבִים כָּל בְּנֵי בְרִיתֶךָ.

(In the next paragraph, when you say the word Blessed, *bend your knees; for* You, *bow at the waist; for* A-donai, *straighten up and continue your prayer.)*

וְכֹל הַחַיִּים יוֹדוּךָ סֶּלָה, וִיהַלְלוּ אֶת שִׁמְךָ בֶּאֱמֶת, הָאֵל יְשׁוּעָתֵנוּ וְעֶזְרָתֵנוּ סֶלָה. בָּרוּךְ אַתָּה יהוה, הַטּוֹב שִׁמְךָ וּלְךָ נָאֶה לְהוֹדוֹת.

HODA'AH - GRATITUDE TO GOD

(In the next paragraph, when you say the words We are grateful to You, *bow at the waist; for* A-donai, *straighten up and continue your prayer.)*

We are grateful to You, because it is You Adonai, Who for all eternity is our God and the God of our forefathers; You are the Rock of our lives and the Shield of our deliverance, from generation to generation.

We thank You and tell of Your praise, for our lives that are given over into Your hand—and for our souls that are in Your trusted care—and for Your miracles that accompany us every day, and for Your wonders and Your benevolence, at all times; evening, and morning and afternoon. You are the One Who is solely good, for Your compassion never ceases; and You are the One Who is solely compassionate, for Your kindness has never stopped; always have we placed our hope in You.

For all this, our King, may Your Name be blessed and extolled constantly and forever.

INSCRIBE FOR A GOOD LIFE . . .

And inscribe for a good life, all the children of Your covenant.

(In the next paragraph, when you say the word Blessed, *bend your knees; for* You, *bow at the waist; for* A-donai, *straighten up and continue your prayer.)*

And everything that is alive will express gratitude to You, forever; and sincerely praise Your Name, the all-powerful God of our salvation and help—forever.

Blessed are You, Adonai, "The Good, Benevolent One" is Your Name, and it is proper to express gratitude to You.

⇝ שָׁלוֹם - PEACE ⇜

(During the morning Amidah prayer, say the paragraph on the right. In the afternoon and evening, say the paragraph on the left.)

(Morning Amidah)

שִׂים שָׁלוֹם, טוֹבָה וּבְרָכָה, חֵן וָחֶסֶד וְרַחֲמִים עָלֵינוּ וְעַל כָּל יִשְׂרָאֵל עַמֶּךָ. בָּרְכֵנוּ אָבִינוּ, כֻּלָּנוּ כְּאֶחָד בְּאוֹר פָּנֶיךָ, כִּי בְאוֹר פָּנֶיךָ נָתַתָּ לָּנוּ, יהוה אֱלֹהֵינוּ, תּוֹרַת חַיִּים וְאַהֲבַת חֶסֶד, וּצְדָקָה, וּבְרָכָה, וְרַחֲמִים, וְחַיִּים, וְשָׁלוֹם. וְטוֹב בְּעֵינֶיךָ לְבָרֵךְ אֶת עַמְּךָ יִשְׂרָאֵל, בְּכָל עֵת וּבְכָל שָׁעָה בִּשְׁלוֹמֶךָ.

(Afternoon and Evening Amidah)

שָׁלוֹם רָב עַל יִשְׂרָאֵל עַמְּךָ תָּשִׂים לְעוֹלָם, כִּי אַתָּה הוּא מֶלֶךְ אָדוֹן לְכָל הַשָּׁלוֹם. וְטוֹב בְּעֵינֶיךָ לְבָרֵךְ אֶת עַמְּךָ יִשְׂרָאֵל בְּכָל עֵת וּבְכָל שָׁעָה בִּשְׁלוֹמֶךָ.

SHALOM - PEACE

(During the morning Amidah prayer, say the paragraph on the left. In the afternoon and evening, say the paragraph on the right.)

(Morning Amidah)

Grant peace, goodness and blessing, favor, loving-kindness and compassion on us and on all the people of Israel, Your nation. Bless us, our Father, all of us together as one, with the spiritual light of Your Presence. For with the light of Your Presence You gave us, Adonai our God, the Torah of life and a love of kindness; moral integrity, blessing, compassion, life and peace. And may it be good in Your eyes to bless Your nation, the people of Israel, at all times and at every hour, with Your Peace.

(Afternoon and Evening Amidah)

Grant abundant peace on the people of Israel, Your nation—forever. For You are King, Master (and Director) of all peace. And may it be good in Your eyes to bless Your nation, the people of Israel, at all times and at every hour, with Your Peace.

בְּסֵפֶר חַיִּים בְּרָכָה וְשָׁלוֹם, וּפַרְנָסָה טוֹבָה, נִזָּכֵר וְנִכָּתֵב לְפָנֶיךָ,
אֲנַחְנוּ וְכָל עַמְּךָ בֵּית יִשְׂרָאֵל, לְחַיִּים טוֹבִים וּלְשָׁלוֹם.

(The next sentence concludes the paragraph of Shalom-Peace. There are two customs regarding the wording of this sentence. While both are acceptable, it is ideal to use the wording that is the custom in your synagogue.)

Version I

בָּרוּךְ אַתָּה יהוה, הַמְבָרֵךְ
אֶת עַמּוֹ יִשְׂרָאֵל בַּשָּׁלוֹם.

Version II

בָּרוּךְ אַתָּה יהוה,
עֹשֵׂה הַשָּׁלוֹם.

(There are also two customs regarding the next phrase. One custom is to say the phrase. The other omits it. While both are acceptable, it is ideal to follow the custom of your family or synagogue.)

יִהְיוּ לְרָצוֹן אִמְרֵי פִי וְהֶגְיוֹן לִבִּי לְפָנֶיךָ, יהוה צוּרִי וְגוֹאֲלִי.

❖ IN THE BOOK OF LIFE . . .

In the book of life, blessing, peace and abundant livelihood, may we be remembered and inscribed before You; we and Your entire nation, the Family of Israel, for good life and for peace.

(The next sentence concludes the paragraph of Shalom-Peace. There are two customs regarding the wording of this sentence. While both are acceptable, it is ideal to use the wording that is the custom in your synagogue.)

Version I	**Version II**
Blessed are You, Adonai, Who blesses His nation, the people of Israel, with peace.	Blessed are You, Adonai, Who makes the peace.

(There are also two customs regarding the next phrase. One custom is to say the phrase. The other omits it. While both are acceptable, it is ideal to follow the custom of your family or synagogue.)

May the words of my mouth, and the thoughts of my heart, be favorably pleasant before You, Adonai, my Rock and my Redeemer.

אֱלֹהַי, נְצוֹר לְשׁוֹנִי מֵרָע, וּשְׂפָתַי מִדַּבֵּר מִרְמָה, וְלִמְקַלְלַי נַפְשִׁי תִדּוֹם, וְנַפְשִׁי כֶּעָפָר לַכֹּל תִּהְיֶה. פְּתַח לִבִּי בְּתוֹרָתֶךָ, וּבְמִצְוֹתֶיךָ תִּרְדּוֹף נַפְשִׁי. וְכֹל הַחוֹשְׁבִים עָלַי רָעָה, מְהֵרָה הָפֵר עֲצָתָם וְקַלְקֵל מַחֲשַׁבְתָּם. עֲשֵׂה לְמַעַן שְׁמֶךָ, עֲשֵׂה לְמַעַן יְמִינֶךָ, עֲשֵׂה לְמַעַן קְדֻשָּׁתֶךָ, עֲשֵׂה לְמַעַן תּוֹרָתֶךָ. לְמַעַן יֵחָלְצוּן יְדִידֶיךָ, הוֹשִׁיעָה יְמִינְךָ וַעֲנֵנִי. יִהְיוּ לְרָצוֹן אִמְרֵי פִי וְהֶגְיוֹן לִבִּי לְפָנֶיךָ, יהוה צוּרִי וְגוֹאֲלִי.

(As you begin the next phrase, bow slightly and take three steps back. When you say the words He who makes peace, *bow to your left; for* may He make peace, *bow to your right; for* And upon all Israel . . . *bow forward.)*

(Bow slightly and take three steps back—)

עֹשֶׂה [הַ]שָּׁלוֹם בִּמְרוֹמָיו, *(Bow to your left)*

הוּא יַעֲשֶׂה שָׁלוֹם עָלֵינוּ, *(Bow to your right)*

וְעַל כָּל יִשְׂרָאֵל. וְאִמְרוּ: אָמֵן. *(Bow forward)*

THE AMIDAH CONCLUDES WITH THIS PARAGRAPH

My God, guard my tongue from evil and my lips from speaking deceitfully. And towards those who curse me, may my soul not respond; and let my soul be (humble) like dust towards everyone. Open my heart to Your Torah and enable my soul to passionately pursue Your commandments. And for all those who plan evil designs against me, quickly void their plots and undermine their intentions. Do this (please) for the sake of Your Name. Do this (please) for the sake of Your right hand. (So that Your Divine involvement in life will be clear to all.) Do this (please) for the sake of (restoring awareness of) Your Holiness. Do this (please) for the sake of (restoring honor to) Your Torah. So that Your beloved (nation) will be freed (from their suffering and oppression)—May Your right hand deliver salvation, and answer me.

May the words of my mouth, and the thoughts of my heart, be favorably pleasant before You, Adonai, my Rock and my Redeemer.

(As you begin the next phrase, bow slightly and take three steps back. When you say the words He who makes peace, *bow to your left; for* may He make peace, *bow to your right; for* And upon all Israel . . . *bow forward.)*

(Bow slightly and take three steps back—)

(Bow to your left) He Who makes peace in His highest realms,
(Bow to your right) May He make peace upon us,
(Bow forward) And upon all the people of Israel, and say, amen.

יהִי רָצוֹן מִלְּפָנֶיךָ, יהוה אֱלֹהֵינוּ וֵאלֹהֵי אֲבוֹתֵינוּ, שֶׁיִּבָּנֶה בֵּית
: הַמִּקְדָּשׁ בִּמְהֵרָה בְיָמֵינוּ, וְתֵן חֶלְקֵנוּ בְּתוֹרָתֶךָ, וְשָׁם נַעֲבָדְךָ
בְּיִרְאָה, כִּימֵי עוֹלָם וּכְשָׁנִים קַדְמוֹנִיּוֹת. וְעָרְבָה לַיהוה מִנְחַת
יְהוּדָה וִירוּשָׁלָיִם, כִּימֵי עוֹלָם וּכְשָׁנִים קַדְמוֹנִיּוֹת.

Closing meditation

When the Jewish nation finally returns home; when Jerusalem and the Temple are rebuilt, when every Jew achieves a sense of personal connection to the Torah—God's instructions for life—and when every Jew has a deep relationship with the Creator, then everything else will fall into place: for us and for the entire world.

With the three steps we took back, we were stepping out of a rarefied dimension of God consciousness, a place where we were literally able to speak to God. Following the closing meditation paragraph, for a few moments, remain standing—still and silent. Let the experience of the Amidah settle into your being, and take it with you—forever.

May it be Your will, Adonai, our God and God of our forefathers, that the holy Temple be rebuilt, speedily in our days; And grant us our personal share in Your Torah, and we will serve You there with reverence, as in the days of antiquity, and in earlier years. Then the offerings of (the people of) Judah and Jerusalem will be pleasantly acceptable to God, as in the days of antiquity, and in earlier years.

According to Jewish tradition, Elijah the Prophet is able to bypass the normal constraints of time. At every *brit mila* (circumcision), a chair is designated as the "Seat of Elijah." On Passover, we place a fifth cup of wine on the Seder table—Elijah's Cup.

Israel ben Eliezer lived from 1700 to 1760. Orphaned at a young age, Israel was raised by the community and later became a tutor to young children. Unbeknownst to those around him, Israel was also a member of a secret society of scholars and master Kabbalists. Eventually, Rabbi Israel ben Eliezer became known as the Baal Shem Tov. He is the founder of the Chassidic movement. Many stories are told of the Baal Shem Tov. Some of these stories are about the mystical visitations of Elijah the Prophet: this is one of them.

Once, shortly before Rosh Hashanah, a student came to the Baal Shem Tov and said that he wanted to meet Elijah the Prophet. The Baal Shem Tov instructed him to travel to a small ramshackle cottage deep in a far away forest. After an arduous three-day journey, he finally arrived. There, the student found only a poor widow and her children. A kind woman, she invited the man to spend Rosh Hashanah with them, though she had barely a piece of bread to offer for the holiday meal. Fortunately, the man had brought food for his journey, and this he shared with the family. For two days, the student anxiously awaited the appearance of Elijah: it never came to be.

Disappointed, the student traveled back to the Baal Shem Tov. The Baal Shem Tov assured his student that Elijah had been there, and that if he would go back for Yom Kippur, he would meet him. Again, the student made the long difficult journey. This time, he arrived shortly before sunset on the eve of Yom Kippur. From inside the home he could hear the children crying bitterly. "Mother, we have nothing at all to eat, how will we prepare for Yom Kippur—we're starving." "Be calm my children," she said, "Just like God sent Elijah the Prophet to visit us for Rosh Hashanah, surely he will do so again." Hearing that, the student knew why the Baal Shem Tov had sent him on the journey.

ABOUT THE AUTHOR

Shimon Apisdorf is an award-winning author whose books have been read by hundreds of thousands of people around the world. His writing is insightful and refreshing, and he is able to make the world of Jewish life and wisdom sparkle with relevance.

Though his heart is in the *Rova*, he currently resides with his wife Miriam, and their children, in Baltimore. The Apisdorfs enjoy long walks by the water, baseball, and backyard barbecues; learning, discussing, and exploring life together; good stories, good music, and sitting in the sukkah.

The Afikim Foundation expresses its thanks to ***Yuval Nadel*** *for the use of his stunning photographs. His book will be a beautiful addition to any Jewish home.*